◉CBS

THE FIRST 50 YEARS

⦿CBS
THE FIRST 50 YEARS

By Tony Chiu
Bruce Pomerantz, Photo Editor

Foreword by Walter Cronkite

CBS

Los Angeles

Publisher: W. Quay Hays
Editorial Director: Peter Hoffman
Editor: Steve Baeck
Art Director: Kurt Wahlner
Designer: Dana Granoski
Production Director: Trudihope Schlomowitz
Prepress Manager: Bill Castillo
Production Assistants: Tom Archibeque,
Dave Chadderdon, Russel Lockwood, Bill Neary
Editorial Assistant: Dominic Friesen
Copy Editor: Carolyn Wendt

Cover concept: Robert Avellan
Jacket design: Dana Granoski

All photographs courtesy of:
The CBS Photo Archive
51 West 52nd Street
New York, New York 10019
Telephone: (212) 975-4475
Fax: (212) 975-9764

For information:
General Publishing Group, Inc.
2701 Ocean Park Boulevard, Suite 140
Santa Monica, CA 90405

Library of Congress Cataloging-in-Publication Data

Chiu, Tony.
    CBS, the first 50 years / by Tony Chiu.
       p.   cm.
    ISBN 1-57544-083-0 (hardcover)
    1. CBS Inc.—History. I. Title
PN1992.92.C38C55 1998
384.55'06573—dc21   98-18445
                                                                                    CIP

Printed in the USA
by RR Donnelly and Sons Company, Inc.
10 9 8 7 6 5 4 3 2 1

General Publishing Group
Los Angeles

Television was the baby of broadcasting in 1948 when William S. Paley announced that on Tuesday, April 6, at 7:00 P.M., "CBS-TV cameras [will] visit the Alvin Theater in New York City to present...actual play scenes and behind-the-scenes glimpses of the Broadway smash hit *Mr. Roberts*, starring Henry Fonda." Calling it an event "of historic importance and exciting promise," Mr. Paley, who 20 years earlier had founded the Columbia Broadcasting System with a group of radio stations, added, "Certainly, one's imagination is stirred by this experimental joining together of the oldest and the newest forms of entertainment art."

Mr. Roberts was the first program broadcast by the CBS Television Network. Of course, the Network wasn't the nation-spanning institution we know. That first show, the company proudly pointed out at the time, "will be sent via the Columbia television network to viewers over 500 miles of the Atlantic seaboard from Boston to Washington."

We at CBS still feel the excitement of that announcement made a half-century ago, and we feel it every day as the heirs and caretakers of that experiment. And as testament, we offer *CBS: The First 50 Years*, a landmark photo-history that captures our American popular culture and the defining world events that riveted the nation—as seen through the lenses of CBS photographers.

For 50 years, the CBS Television Network has been the source of broadcast news, from Edward R. Murrow to Dan Rather; from *Harvest of Shame* to *60 Minutes*; from Vietnam to the Moon. The channel for variety entertainment, from Ed Sullivan's *Toast of the Town* to the *Late Show with David Letterman*. A theater for challenging drama, from *Studio One* to *Chicago Hope*. The home of family comedy, from *The Goldbergs* to *All in the Family* to *Everybody Loves Raymond*. The screen for television movies, from *The Autobiography of Miss Jane Pittman* to *Lonesome Dove* to *The Last Don*. A range for Westerns, from *Gunsmoke* to *Dr. Quinn, Medicine Woman*. A break in a busy day, from *Guiding Light* to *The Young and the Restless*. A magic box for children, from *Captain Kangaroo* to Charlie Brown. A field of green, from The Masters to the National Football League.

In this book you'll find the headline-makers of a half-century, the faces of CBS's first 50 years, as well as ordinary people who have been brushed—or crushed—by events. Each photograph evokes a shared American memory; many stir our private thoughts. For the thousands of us who have been part of the CBS Family and for the millions of you who have watched our work, each picture is a mirror of our history, our foibles and fashions, our fun and games—our nation and our lives.

Michael Jordan
Chairman and Chief Executive Officer
CBS Corporation

This book is a tribute to everyone who has worked at CBS in the last half-century in front of the cameras or behind, on soundstages and at ballparks, and to those who risked their lives covering the news. It is also a bow to the more than 200 television stations across America that carry and contribute to CBS's programming and news coverage.

After all, everything began with the local station. The Columbia Broadcasting System started in 1928 with the linking of 16 independent radio stations. Three years later, an experimental television station in New York started to beam programming to a handful of viewers gathered around their little round screens. In 1941, WCBS-TV New York went on the air once a week with programs for another tiny audience.

The CBS Television Network was launched in 1948. It consisted of five stations delivering a flickering black-and-white signal. But people wanted those pictures of news, entertainment, special events, and sports, and television sets began to sell. Since then, the images and words have come to you through rabbit ears, roof antennas, wired hookups, and now satellites. Today the sound is in stereo, the pictures in stunning color—but however we deliver it, a network is still a group of stations, and the CBS you know is reflected by the local outlet in your hometown.

In our half-century, the Network has brought the world into local communities, and the stations have reflected back their local concerns. That dialogue is reflected in CBS's long history of programming innovation and its dedication to news and to progress in the communities we serve.

Each photograph in this extraordinary book will trigger a second memory—of the local kid's show host who came on after *Captain Kangaroo*, the local anchor who introduced Douglas Edwards, the neighbor's kid who said the darndest thing to Art Linkletter, the friend's daughter who danced on *The Carol Burnett Show*, the high school buddy who served in Vietnam. Or of the local broadcaster who left town to join the Network—like Dan Rather and Jim Nantz and David Letterman.

You saw it on your local station when Mary moved in downstairs from Rhoda; when Kristin shot J.R.; when *M*A*S*H* said goodbye or *Touched By An Angel* said hello; when the news came from Dallas or Saigon or Oklahoma City. And because there was a CBS Television Network, we all experienced it together.

Mel Karmazin
President and Chief Operating Officer
CBS Corporation

Many people still recall with amazement the day Edward R. Murrow shared with the American public simultaneous real-time pictures of the Golden Gate and Brooklyn Bridges—a truly remarkable, almost unthinkable split-screen image in a country just beginning to take center stage as a world power. It was also a defining moment for a medium, television, that would inform, entertain, and, indeed, unify us all.

Since those early days of William Paley and the other titans who ushered in this Age of Communication, CBS has provided viewers with an unparalleled parade of American icons. The stars pictured in this book are CBS to the billions of viewers who have watched our programs through the years

On every page you'll find a snapshot of a shared moment in this nation's history. And these static images cannot help but bring to mind very real and very moving pictures in the private newsreels we all replay.

If you remember that day in 1951 when Atlantic and Pacific appeared together, live, on your screen, you'll remember not only the two coasts but also the man who brought them to you. Similarly, for millions, President John F. Kennedy's death was a moment permanently etched by Walter Cronkite choking back his emotions. Where were you the day Neil Armstrong stepped onto the moon and the day *Challenger* failed? The day a U.S. president resigned and the day the citizens of Berlin hammered down their hated Wall? The day Diana Spencer married a prince of the realm and the day the world mourned her passing?

Page through this book, find an image, and recall a television moment: Lucy stuffing chocolates into her mouth. Ralph Kramden threatening to send Alice "to the moon." Ed Sullivan bringing on Elvis and the Beatles. Marshall Dillon facing down the latest villain in Dodge City. Rod Serling leading us on a weekly journey into the unknown. Dick Van Dyke tripping over the living room ottoman. The Clampetts rolling into Beverly Hills. Mary Tyler Moore gleefully tossing her hat into the air. Kojak sucking the lollipop. Carol Burnett tugging on her earlobe. Carroll O'Connor and Rob Reiner trying to squeeze through the door at the same time. John-Boy intoning his "good-nights" as the lights click off on Walton's Mountain. The 4077th M.A.S.H. unit operating while cracking wise. J.R. scheming. Angela Lansbury sniffing out clues. Murphy Brown grousing. David Letterman stepping gingerly through his Stupid Pet Tricks segment. Ray Romano trying to get a life of his own.

But enough words. Ours is a medium of images, and I now invite you to relive some of the most wonderful images from CBS's first 50 years. Enjoy the show as the television memories begin to unfold in your mind.

Leslie Moonves
President and Chief Executive Officer
CBS Television

Foreword

When William S. Paley moved his highly successful radio network into television the world was a half-century younger than it is today. And what a different world it was:

As that year of 1948 opened there was no Scrabble, deodorant soap, or McDonald's; the super-highway system that would spread the cities out into the countryside and give birth to the mall civilization was still a dream; a jet plane had not yet crossed the Atlantic; and only the readers of the *New York Daily News* had ever heard of columnist Ed Sullivan.

Television itself was just barely out of the experimental stage, there were an estimated one million sets in the whole country, and the network signal was still several years away from being distributed nationwide.

And one of the most successful dramas of the year was Jean Anouilh's *Cry of the Peacock*, which had nothing to do with a famous network rivalry.

The advent of television came with the thunderous roar of an avalanche that forever changed the landscape of our very being. The whole population of the entertainment world seemed suddenly to flee out the stage door to find sanctuary in the living rooms of America.

Just as suddenly, the people's relationship to the world around them was forever altered. News no longer would be defined by still pictures and printed words. Like the singers, dancers, acrobats, ventriloquists, and actors, those who made the news appeared right there in the magic box. The leaders of nations spoke of their aspirations, our politicians of their ambitions.

History came tumbling out of the tube. Residents of those few cities that were interconnected with the networks that first year got an extraordinary lesson in the workings of our democracy. They were taken to a seat in the convention hall where the Republican and Democratic parties met in quadrennial convention. It was an unforgettable civics lesson—a pure and unadulterated view of the chaos out of which we selected our presidential candidates.

Comparatively few saw those 1948 conventions and few of the party leaders understood the impact that television would have. That recognition came four years later when millions of viewers watched this almost incredible show of democracy in the raw, guided through the convention process by network commentators.

Leaders of both parties, just four years after Bill Paley had put CBS TV on the air, vowed to try to harness this communication Goliath and the practice of politics was forever changed. The debate as to the effect of the intricate relationship of politics and television is undecided and perhaps will never be as television has become the essential communications link between the government, the parties, and the people. Those of special interests, whatever their cause, will attempt to use television, and responsible television journalists will keep their guard up against being used, and it probably forever will be thus.

In other aspects, television's news coverage has become truly and remarkably global in this half century. Technical developments—primarily near-miniature cameras and satellite transmission—have truly made the world a global village. We now watch our neighbors deep in the once distant continents as they rejoice over local successes or, far too often, suffer the tragedies of natural disaster or internecine bloodshed. Even Paley perhaps could not have foreseen that television would bring to all of us the lesson that human beings, even those we had once considered the most exotic, share far more in common than we ever had believed. In that lesson there is at least a glimmer of hope that we will someday find the key to international amity.

And, of course, the same is true of our own communities. Television news brought home as nothing else ever had the horrors of racial segregation and inequality of both opportunity and treatment. History certainly will judge television as key to the success, although still incomplete, of the civil rights revolution of this last half-century.

Meanwhile, on the entertainment front, television has played a combined role of reflecting, leading, and accelerating the changes in our culture and our very morality. The exact mix of these various effects, the formula of change, probably is impossible to determine. Certainly the simultaneous exposure of every cultural whim and fad in every American home—and, yes, those around the globe—has had a powerful influence and defied any resistance that might have been occasioned in section or region in the days of slower transmission of ideas and movements.

How much television has led such cultural changes or simply reflected them is too moot for discussion in the limited space here. Let us be satisfied with the knowledge that this interrelationship is inseparable.

Television has had one major influence on the value of which sociologists disagree. Probably more even than the super-highway, jet travel, or wartime mixing, it has homogenized America. Our patterns of speech and behavior that once were instantly recognizable by geographical location now are almost indistinguishable. Southerner and Middle-Westerner speak with a single accent—or, in effect, no accent—and act and react with a uniformity unique to our wide country.

It has been some half-century! Those of us who have been lucky enough to have a close association with CBS through these years are proud to be part of our company. What Bill Paley founded and the extraordinary Frank Stanton helped develop became known, with full justice, as The Tiffany Network.

CBS indeed is a diamond whose many facets reflect in glistening intensity the last half of the Twentieth Century and the end of a millennium.

—Walter Cronkite

tel•e•vi•sion, n. A system for reproducing an actual or recorded scene at a distance on a screen.

"There's a good deal in common between the mind's eye and the TV screen, and though the TV set has all too often been the boobtube, it could be, it can be, the box of dreams."

— *Ursula K. LeGuin*, 1989

Harry S. Truman defeats Thomas E. Dewey for the presidency. Congress passes the Marshall Plan to aid reconstruction of Europe. Nationhood: Israel. India's Mohandas K. Gandhi, 78, is shot dead by a Hindu extremist. John Bardeen, 40, Walter Brattain, 46, and William Shockley, 38, invent the transistor. America has 970,000 TV sets in use.

Premiering series: *Kukla, Fran and Ollie* (NBC); *Lamp Unto My Feet* (CBS); *Studio One* (CBS); *Talent Scouts* (with Arthur Godfrey, CBS); *Ted Mack's Original Amateur Hour* (DUMONT); *The Texaco Star Theater* (with Milton Berle, NBC); *Toast of the Town* (CBS).

Movies: *Hamlet* (with Laurence Olivier; Oscar); *Red River*; *The Red Shoes*; *The Search*; *The Treasure of the Sierra Madre*.

Songs: "Buttons and Bows" (Dinah Shore); "Nature Boy" (Nat "King" Cole); "Red Roses for a Blue Lady" (Vaughn Monroe); "Tennessee Waltz" (Cowboy Copas).

Books: *Cry, the Beloved Country* (Alan Paton); *Economics* (Paul Samuelson's textbook); *The Naked and the Dead* (Norman Mailer); *The Plague* (Albert Camus); *Sexual Behavior in the Human Male* (Alfred Kinsey).

Died: director Sergei Eisenstein, 50; director D.W. Griffith, 73; baseball's Babe Ruth, 53; aviator Orville Wright, 77.

Debuts: the 33$\frac{1}{3}$ rpm long-playing record (invented by CBS engineer Peter Goldmark); Scrabble; V-8 juice; Nestlé's Quik; *Pogo* (by cartoonist Walt Kelly, 35).

Newspaper columnist **Ed Sullivan**, 46, wasn't exactly telegenic. And CBS budgeted a munificent $1,375 for his first *Toast of the Town* variety hour, headlined by Dean Martin and Jerry Lewis. But Sullivan, here with the **June Taylor Dancers**, was to rule Sunday nights for 23 years by presenting a parade of singers and dancing bears and ventriloquists and comedians and jugglers and ballet troupes—and much, much more.

Two years after starting *Talent Scouts* on CBS radio, **Arthur Godfrey** transferred his show to television. Among the winners, as chosen by an audience applause meter: the McGuire Sisters and Pat Boone. Among the finalists: Tony Bennett and Rosemary Clooney. Among those who flunked auditions: Elvis Presley and Buddy Holly.

Sports was a television mainstay from the first, though for technical reasons few events were broadcast live unless they took place near New York City, where the networks were based. CBS's exclusive coverage of racing's Triple Crown—captured by Citation, here in its stretch drive at the Belmont Stakes—was presented on film.

Not content to merely televise movie newsreels, as two other networks were doing, CBS created a 15-minute studio-based newscast. Its first anchor: **Douglas Edwards**, who had a daily news show on WCBS-TV in New York. Five nights after the photo below was taken, Edwards used the same set to launch *The CBS Evening News*.

After covering the Republican and Democratic conventions gavel-to-gavel, CBS News pre-empted its primetime shows on November 2 to report the vote. It was an Election Night to remember. Tallying was slow in the pre-computer age; but when the returns were in, Harry Truman had engineered the greatest political upset of the 20th century by defeating Tom Dewey.

• • • • • • • • • •

WILLIAM S. PALEY

Founder of CBS TV, on the infant medium:

"We [soon] learned that creating television programs was a dynamic art with a life of its own. Producers had to find new variations on old forms. What worked on radio or on the stage or even in the movies did not necessarily work on the small screen."

The U.S. and 11 European nations form the North Atlantic Treaty Organization to counter Communism. South Africa legalizes apartheid. Nationhood: People's Republic of China (proclaimed by Mao Tse-tung, 56); Indonesia (gaining independence from the Netherlands); Eire (Republic of Ireland); East and West Germanys. TV sets in use: 1 million.

Premiering series: *Arthur Godfrey and His Friends* (CBS); *Captain Video* (DUMONT); *The Fred Waring Show* (CBS); *The Goldbergs* (CBS); *Hopalong Cassidy* (NBC); *The Life of Riley* (with Jackie Gleason, NBC); *The Lone Ranger* (ABC); *Mama* (CBS).

Movies: *Adam's Rib*; *All the King's Men* (Oscar); De Sica's *The Bicycle Thief*; *The Third Man*; *Twelve O'Clock High*.

Songs: "Baby, It's Cold Outside" (Esther Williams and Ricardo Montalban); "Mule Train" (Frankie Laine); "Rudolph the Red-Nosed Reindeer" (Gene Autry).

Books: *The Lottery* (Shirley Jackson); *1984* (George Orwell); *The Second Sex* (Simone de Beauvoir); *The Sheltering Sky* (Paul Bowles).

Died: bluesman Huddie "Leadbelly" Ledbetter, 60; *Gone with the Wind* author Margaret Mitchell, 49 (run over by a car in Atlanta); dancer Bill "Bojangles" Robinson, 71; composer Richard Straus, 85.

Debuts: the 17-team National Basketball Association; 45 rpm records (developed by RCA); Silly Putty.

Who said comedy isn't pretty? *The Ed Wynn Show*, starring the legendary vaudevillian (far right, in a sketch with, from left to right, **Marty Katz**, **Maxine Semon**, and **Garry Moore**), was the first CBS variety program to originate in Los Angeles. It aired only one season, but won an Emmy for Best Live Show.

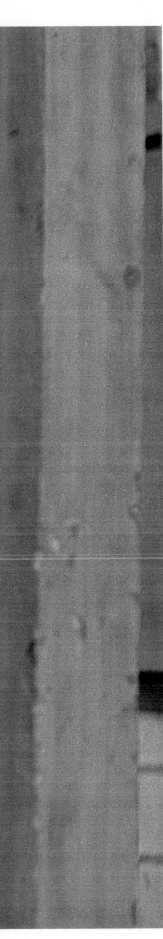

The life of the Hansens, a Norwegian family in early 20th-century San Francisco, had been the basis of a book and a hit play and movie (both titled *I Remember Mama*) before CBS created the half-hour drama *Mama*. In the title role was stage actress **Peggy Wood**; youngest daughter Dagmar was originally portrayed by **Iris Mann**.

For one month, CBS devoted three hours per day to live broadcasts of the United Nations General Assembly from its temporary headquarters in Flushing Meadows, New York. Founded in 1945 by 51 member nations, the U.N. would move into its permanent home, overlooking New York's East River, in 1952.

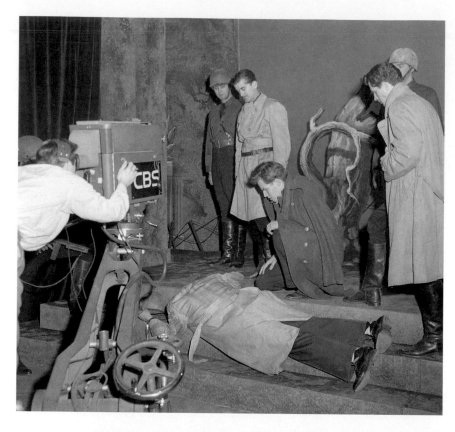

Studio One's live version of Shakespeare's *Julius Caesar*—condensed to fit a one-hour time slot and done in modern dress to save on costumes—proved so popular that the cast was quickly reunited for a repeat performance. Yes, the young Marc Antony kneeling over the corpse is 24-year-old **Charlton Heston** (né Charles Carter), seven years before his breakthrough movie, *The Ten Commandments*.

World War I was still raging when **Fred Waring** organized his first band. By the time *The Fred Waring Show* debuted, he had also become the owner of a prominent resort in Pennsylvania and developed the Waring blender. Among the featured singers on his hour-long musical: Hugh Brannum, later Captain Kangaroo's sidekick, Mr. Green Jeans.

In
Their
Own
Words

· · · · · · · · · ·

GERTRUDE BERG

Star of The Gold-bergs, *on why a show about a Jewish family from the Bronx was a hit on CBS radio for 20 years before becoming TV's top-rated sitcom in its first season:*

"Ours was never a show that made jokes about people. The humor comes out of life and the warmth of the characters."

North Korea invades South Korea. After Foreign Service officer Alger Hiss is convicted of perjury in a spy ring case, Senator Joseph McCarthy claims the State Department is rife with Communists. The anonymously published book *Red Channels* claims the entertainment industry is, too.

Premiering series: *Beat the Clock* (CBS); *Beulah* (ABC); *The Burns and Allen Show* (CBS); *The Cisco Kid* (SYND); *The Gene Autry Show* (CBS); *Racket Squad* (SYND); *Tom Corbett, Space Cadet* (CBS); *Truth or Consequences* (CBS); *What's My Line?* (CBS); *You Bet Your Life* (with Groucho Marx, NBC); *Your Show of Shows* (with Sid Caesar, NBC).

Movies: *All About Eve* (Oscar); *The Asphalt Jungle*; De Santis's *Bitter Rice*; *Born Yesterday*; *Cinderella*; *Sunset Boulevard*.

Songs: "Be My Love" (Mario Lanza); "Goodnight, Irene" (The Weavers); "Tennessee Waltz" (Patti Page); "The Third Man Theme" (Anton Karas).

Books: *Betty Crocker's Picture Cookbook*; *Kon-Tiki* (Thor Heyerdahl); *The Lion, the Witch and the Wardrobe* (C.S. Lewis); *Pippi Longstocking* (Astrid Lindgren).

Died: *Tarzan* creator Edgar Rice Burroughs, 75; dancer Vaslav Nijinsky, 60; writer George Orwell, 46; playwright George Bernard Shaw, 94; composer Kurt Weill, 50.

Debuts: Xerox copier; contact lenses; credit card (invented by Diners Club); *Peanuts* (by cartoonist Charles Schulz, 27).

Gene Autry, Hollywood's top-grossing cowboy crooner, giddyapped onto the small screen (with sidekick **Pat Buttram** and horse **Champion**) a year before archrival Roy Rogers. Both were beaten to the draw by another Western hero, but Hopalong Cassidy mostly recycled his old Saturday-matinee four-reelers; each episode of *The Gene Autry Show* was shot for television.

The top news story of the year broke on June 25 when North Korea, encouraged by Communist China, invaded South Korea. Two weeks later the United Nations voted to muster a peacekeeping force under U.S. command. Air sorties by American warplanes helped contain the North Koreans until mid-September, when troops led by General Douglas MacArthur began a counterattack.

Forty-year-old **Dick Foran** was a durable B-movie star when he was teamed with an ingenue from Philadelphia half his age in the *Studio One* production *The Kill*. Two years later, after her first starring movie role, opposite Gary Cooper in *High Noon*, **Grace Kelly** was on Hollywood's A-list.

A quarter-century after meeting on the vaudeville circuit, **Gracie Allen** and **George Burns** brought their act to television. Each episode of *The Burns and Allen Show*, on which they portrayed themselves, ended with an homage to their roots, a bit of curtain-call schtick. The curtain came down on the series in 1958 when Allen, then 52, decided to retire from show business.

Testing taste buds was a relatively tidy *Beat the Clock* stunt; for prizes of less than $100, many contestants endured whipped-cream dousings. **Bud Collyer** hosted the primetime run through 1958 and a daytime version from 1958 to 1961. Collyer also specialized in supplying the voices of superheroes (Superman on radio in the 1940s, Batman on the 1968–70 CBS animated series).

Fifteen months after DuMont launched *Captain Video*, CBS responded with *Tom Corbett, Space Cadet.* Set in the 24th century, the thrice-weekly 15-minute show starred **Frankie Thomas** as Corbett, here being shown the door by one of his Space Academy instructors, **Margaret Garland.**

. . . .

JACK BENNY

On entering TV cautiously (The Jack Benny Program aired only four times during the 1950–51 season):

"Television will be the world's most wonderful medium of entertainment. However, I think radio will go on and on. Eventually a good radio show will have a better chance than a mediocre TV show —and vice versa."

1951

1919

General Douglas MacArthur is stripped of command in Korea by President Truman for unauthorized policy statements. Julius Rosenberg, 32, and his wife, Ethel, 35, are sentenced to die for passing atomic secrets to Moscow. Bobby Thomson's last-out homer sends his New York Giants into the World Series (which features rookies Willie Mays, 20, of the Giants and Mickey Mantle, 19, of the Yankees). TV sets in use: 10.6 million.

Premiering series: *The Amos and Andy Show* (CBS); *Dragnet* (NBC); *I Love Lucy* (CBS); *Love of Life* (CBS); *Mr. Wizard* (NBC); *The Roy Rogers Show* (NBC); *Search for To-morrow* (CBS); *See It Now* (CBS); *Sky King* (NBC); *Strike It Rich* (CBS); *Superman* (SYND).

Movies: *The African Queen*; *An American in Paris* (Oscar); Kurosawa's *Rashomon*; *Quo Vadis?*; *A Streetcar Named Desire*.

Songs: "Chains of Love" (Joe Turner); "Come On-a My House" (Rosemary Clooney); "Cry" (Johnnie Ray); "Kisses Sweeter Than Wine" (The Weavers).

Books: *The Caine Mutiny* (Herman Wouk); *The Catcher in the Rye* (J.D. Salinger); *From Here to Eternity* (James Jones); *The Origins of Totalitarianism* (Hannah Arendt).

Died: showgirl Fanny Brice, 60; publisher William R. Hearst, 90; cereal maker W.K. Kellogg, 91; novelist Sinclair Lewis, 65.

Debuts: CBS's "Eye" logo; area codes; UNIVAC mainframe computer; *Dennis the Menace* (by cartoonist Hank Ketcham, 30).

With **Vivian Vance**, **Lucille Ball**, **Desi Arnaz**, and **William Frawley** around, something fishy was usually afoot on *I Love Lucy*. Ball, at 40 a veteran of three dozen Hollywood comedies, made two demands when asked to do a televersion of her radio hit, *My Favorite Husband*. She wanted real-life hubby Arnaz to costar, and the series to originate from Los Angeles. To ensure picture quality, *Lucy* became the first filmed sitcom—and thus the first available for reruns.

The residents of Henderson began their *Search for Tomorrow* on September 3 (from right: **Mary Stuart**, who survived the soap's entire 35-year run; **Bess Johnson**; **Lynn Loring**; **Sara Anderson**; **Cliff Hall**, and **John Sylvester**). Other then-unsung actors who appeared in the 9,000-plus episodes: Robby Benson, Jill Clayburgh, Kevin Kline, Don Knotts, Hal Linden, Wayne Rogers, and Susan Sarandon.

On *Strike It Rich*, **Warren Hull** coaxed
contestants to share their sorrows: vanished
spouses, sick kids, lost jobs. Next came the
"Heart Line" segment, on which viewers
phoned in donations. When needy families
desperate to become contestants began
arriving in New York on one-way tickets, the
city's Welfare Department labeled the game
show "a national disgrace."

After a 23-year radio run, on which the lead
characters were played by whites, *The Amos
and Andy Show* (from left, **Spencer Williams** as Andy, **Alvin Childress** as Amos, and
Tim Moore as "Kingfish" Stevens) became the
second series with an all-black cast (after
DuMont's short-lived *The Laytons*). In 1966,
after protests by civil-rights groups, CBS with-
drew it from syndication. The next all-black
network show: 1972's *Sanford and Son*.

CBS News's live coverage of Senate investigations chaired by Tennessee's Estes Kefauver alerted many to the pervasiveness of organized crime in America. Most powerful of the mobs identified: a group rooted in Sicily known as the Mafia.

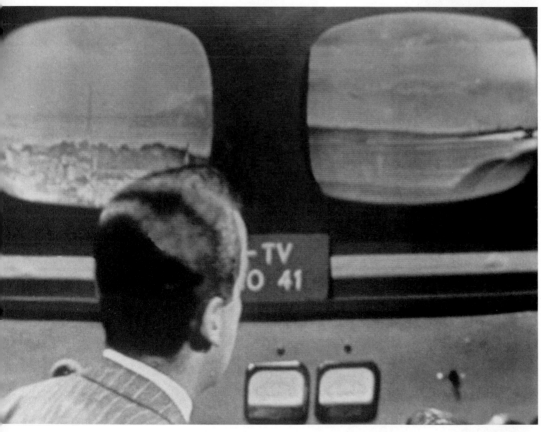

See It Now made its debut on November 18 with an historic split-screen shot: at left was the Golden Gate Bridge and on the right the Brooklyn Bridge. It was the first live commercial coast-to-coast broadcast. **Edward R. Murrow**'s weekly current events program was quickly moved from dinnertime on Sunday to primetime on Tuesday.

EDWARD R. MURROW

On television:

"[It] can teach, it can illuminate; yes, it can even inspire. But it can do so only to the extent that humans are determined [to pursue] it to those ends. Otherwise, it is merely wires and lights in a box. There is a great and perhaps decisive battle to be fought against ignorance, intolerance, and indifference. This weapon of television could be useful."

Dwight D. Eisenhower defeats Adlai E. Stevenson for the presidency. The U.S. detonates the first hydrogen bomb, obliterating the Pacific island of Elugelab. Sixteen-year-old Hussein I claims Jordan's throne. After sex-change surgery in Denmark, George Jorgensen, 26, returns to America as Christine.

Premiering series: *The Adventures of Ozzie and Harriet* (ABC); *Art Linkletter's House Party* (CBS); *The Guiding Light* (CBS); *I've Got a Secret* (CBS); *Mr. and Mrs. North* (CBS); *Mr. Peepers* (NBC); *Omnibus* (CBS); *Our Miss Brooks* (CBS); *The Red Buttons Show* (CBS); *This Is Your Life* (NBC); *Today* (NBC).

Movies: Clement's *Forbidden Games*; *The Greatest Show on Earth* (Oscar); *High Noon*; *Singin' in the Rain*; *This Is Cinerama*.

Songs: "Blue Tango" (Leroy Anderson); "Don't Let the Stars Get in Your Eyes" (Perry Como); "Goin' Home" (Fats Domino); "Your Cheatin' Heart" (Hank Williams).

Books: *Charlotte's Web* (E.B. White); *The Diary of a Young Girl* (Anne Frank); *The Invisible Man* (Ralph Ellison); *The Natural* (Bernard Malamud); *The Power of Positive Thinking* (Norman Vincent Peale).

Died: educator Maria Montessori, 81; Argentinian First Lady Eva "Evita" Perón, 33; philosopher George Santayana, 88.

Debuts: commercial jet service (inaugural flight: BOAC, London to Johannesburg); pocket-sized transistor radio (by Sony); *Mad* magazine; Mr. Potato Head.

Jackie Gleason spent 1949 in an NBC sitcom (the first *Life of Riley*) and 1950–51 in a DuMont variety hour (*Cavalcade of Stars*). Then he switched networks again, and it was Away We Go—starting with *The Jackie Gleason Show*, the Great One would be part of CBS's primetime lineup for the next 18 years.

26 / CBS: 1952

When *Our Miss Brooks* made the jump from radio to TV, the sitcom took along most of its original cast, including star **Eve Arden** (née Eunice Quedens, right), **Richard Crenna** (left), and **Gloria McMillan**; only **Robert Rockwell** was new to the televersion. Arden, the veteran of 50-plus movies, won an Emmy in 1953 for her portrayal of the wisecracking English teacher.

Fifteen years before Congress created PBS, culture on TV meant a 90-minute Sunday potpourri titled *Omnibus*. Host Alistair Cooke introduced scenes from plays (like *The Trial of Mr. Pickwick*, below), operas, symphonies, Kabuki, ballet, and even, in 1954, an early documentary by a French oceanographer named Jacques Cousteau.

Of the radio soap operas transplanted to TV, only *The Guiding Light* was an unqualified success (turning 46 in 1998). In addition to charter cast members (from left) **Lyle Sudrow**, **Jone Allison**, **Herb Nelson**, and **Susan Douglas**, regulars have included Kevin Bacon, Sandy Dennis, Barnard Hughes, James Earl Jones, Joe Lando, Christopher Walken, Billy Dee Williams, JoBeth Williams, and Ian Ziering.

Nine weeks after being named Dwight Eisenhower's running mate, Senator **Richard M. Nixon**, 39, went on TV to explain away $18,000 in undeclared donations from wealthy Californians. The money will "permit me to carry on my fight against Communism," he said, adding that one secret gift was "a little cocker spaniel dog" his young daughter Tricia had already named Checkers.

An established radio variety show host, **Art Linkletter** made the jump to television with ease. The signature segment of each afternoon's *Art Linkletter's House Party* came when he reaffirmed that indeed, kids say the darndest things.

ARTHUR GODFREY

On winding up with the year's Nos. 2– and 3– ranked primetime programs, plus a new daytime show that was a simulcast of his daily radio hour:

"Television was really kind of a joke on me. The last thing in the world I expected was for it to supplant radio. Only the visionaries knew that, and I certainly wasn't one of them."

29

An armistice signed at Panmunjon ends the Korean War. Scientists Francis Crick and Maurice Wilkins of England and James Watson of America discover the double-helix structure of DNA. Edmund Hillary of New Zealand and Tenzing Norkay of Nepal scale 29,023-foot Mount Everest.

Premiering series : *General Electric Theater* (CBS); *The Life of Riley* (with William Bendix, NBC); *Life with Father* (CBS); *Person to Person* (CBS); *Private Secretary* (CBS); *The Red Skelton Show* (CBS); *Topper* (CBS); *Winky-Dink and You* (CBS); *You Are There* (CBS).

Movies: *Bwana Devil* (first 3-D picture); *From Here to Eternity* (Oscar); *Peter Pan*; *Roman Holiday*; *Shane*; *Stalag 17*.

Songs: "Doggie in the Window" (Patti Page); "Stranger in Paradise" (Tony Bennett); "That's Amore" (Dean Martin); "Vaya con Dios" (Les Paul and Mary Ford).

Books: *Fahrenheit 451* (Ray Bradbury); *Sexual Behavior in the Human Female* (Alfred Kinsey); *A Stillness at Appomattox* (Bruce Caton).

Died: playwright Eugene O'Neill, 65; composer Sergei Prokofiev, 61; Soviet dictator Joseph Stalin, 73; athlete Jim Thorpe, 64; singer Hank Williams, 29.

Debuts: aerosol-spray nozzle (invented by Robert Aplanalp); Chevrolet Corvette; *TV Guide*; *Playboy*; Agent 007 (in Ian Fleming's *Casino Royale*); the Church of Scientology (founded by L. Ron Hubbard, 44).

Red Skelton tried out a new gag on foil **Johnny Carson** (one of his first TV writers). Most of Skelton's familiar comic personas—the Mean Widdle Kid, Cauliflower McPugg, Clem Kaddiddlehopper—were lifted from his long-run radio series. The one character created just for *The Red Skelton Show*: hobo Freddie the Freeloader, whose skits were performed in pantomime.

Remember the days when the head of a talent agency (a) wore untrendy suits and (b) rewarded his *Private Secretary* for meddling in his personal life? Without a hint of on-air romance to thicken the plot, **Ann Sothern** and **Don Porter** kept the sitcom going for four seasons, twice placing in Nielsen's Top 20.

Before **Jack Barry** hosted game shows like *Concentration* and *Twenty-One*, he led kids through the interactive *Winky-Dink and You*. The show's cartoon star often needed a ladder or a bridge to continue its adventure, so the action would pause while the viewer drew the required prop. A clear-plastic Winky-Dink screen-saver was for sale by mail, but a lot of kids just crayoned the tube.

In an era of rabbit-ear antennas and iffy reception, the only welcome on-screen ghosts were *Topper*'s **Anne Jeffries** and **Robert Sterling** (in the roles originated in the 1937 movie by Constance Bennett and Cary Grant). The couple's afterlife mission: loosen up the proper banker who bought their old house, **Leo G. Carroll**'s Cosmo Topper.

Fifteen months after the death of her father, King George VI, from cigarette-related cancer, **Elizabeth II** was crowned Queen of England. In the pre-satellite, pre-jet age, CBS News chartered planes to fly film of the ceremony across the Atlantic—editing the footage onboard—and was able to air a report nationally less than 12 hours later.

Leon Ames and **Lurene Tuttle** were raising four redheaded sons in *Life with Father*, a sitcom set in New York City in the 1880s. It was based on Clarence Day's best-selling memoirs, which had previously spawned a Broadway hit and a 1947 movie starring William Powell and Irene Dunne.

. . . .

LUCILLE BALL

Here at home with Desi Arnaz, on working while carrying Desi Jr. (coincidentally born the same day, January 19, that she "delivered" Little Ricky on I Love Lucy):

"I loved doing all those pregnant shows. I was so damned happy— just floating on a cloud—and I think the way I felt came across on the film."

In *Brown* v. *Board of Eduction.*, the U.S. Supreme Court rules that racially "(s)eparated educational facilities are inherently unequal." Vietnam is divided into North (run by Ho Chi Minh) and South (run by Ngo Dinh Diem). Britain ends its 72-year occupation of Egypt. England's Roger Bannister, 25, becomes the first human known to run a mile in less than four minutes. TV sets in use: 27.3 million.

Premiering series : *Captain Midnight* (CBS); *December Bride* (CBS); *Disneyland* (ABC); *Face the Nation* (CBS); *Father Knows Best* (CBS); *Lassie* (CBS); *The Lineup* (CBS); *Medic* (NBC); *Rin Tin Tin* (ABC); *The Tonight Show* (with Steve Allen, NBC).

Movies: *The Caine Mutiny*; *On the Waterfront* (Oscar); *Rear Window*; Kurosawa's *The Seven Samurai*; *A Star Is Born* (with Judy Garland).

Songs: "Earth Angel" (The Penguins); "Sh-Boom" (The Crew-Cuts); "Three Coins in the Fountain" (The Four Aces); "Work With Me, Annie" (Hank Ballard).

Books: *The Long Goodbye* (Raymond Chandler); *Lord of the Flies* (William Golding); *The Lord of the Rings* (J.R.R. Tolkien).

Died: physicist Enrico Fermi, 53; film pioneer Auguste Lumière, 91; artist Henri Matisse, 84; mathematician Alan Turing, 42.

Debuts: polio vaccine (developed by Dr. Jonas Salk); franchised McDonald's hamburger stands; *Sports Illustrated*; frozen TV dinners (Swanson).

Who needed 101 dalmatians when you had (from left) **Pal**, **Young Laddie**, **Lassie**, **Old Laddie**, and **Lassie Jr.**? The five collies, all male, collectively portrayed the canine hero who had already starred in a quartet of movies, two with Elizabeth Taylor. TV's *Lassie* would have almost as many owners as a cat has lives: six masters during the show's 22-year run, the first 17 of which were on CBS.

From his mountaintop jetport, *Captain Midnight* emerged every Saturday morning to fight evil. Originally a long-run radio serial, the televersion starred **Richard Webb** (right) and **Sid Melton** as his low-watt sidekick, Iggy Mudd. Each show ended with the hero spelling out an encrypted message that kids at home could unscramble with an official Secret Squadron ring (available by mail from sponsor Ovaltine).

Hollywood veteran **Spring Byington** was a widow whom on-screen daughter **Frances Rafferty** constantly sought to make a *December Bride.* None of the suitors ever worked out. Nor did many of the sitcom's culinary efforts, like this try at a Chinese dish, pressed duck.

Studio One earned three Emmys for its live production of *Twelve Angry Men*: Reginald Rose for script, Franklin J. Schaffner for direction, and **Robert Cummings** (back row, second from left) for Best Actor in the role Henry Fonda would recreate in the 1957 Hollywood version. Among the other jurors debating a street punk's guilt were **Edward Arnold** (back, fourth from left), **Norman Fell** (front left), and **Franchot Tone** (front, third from left).

Joseph R. McCarthy's pursuit of Communists in high U.S. government circles had already given name to an era when Edward R. Murrow devoted two *See It Now* shows to chronicling the Wisconsin politician's inconsistencies and lies. Appearing live to rebut, the senator, 46, chose not to set the record straight but to denounce Murrow as "the leader and cleverest of the jackal pack." Eight months later McCarthy was censured by the Senate; three years later he was dead.

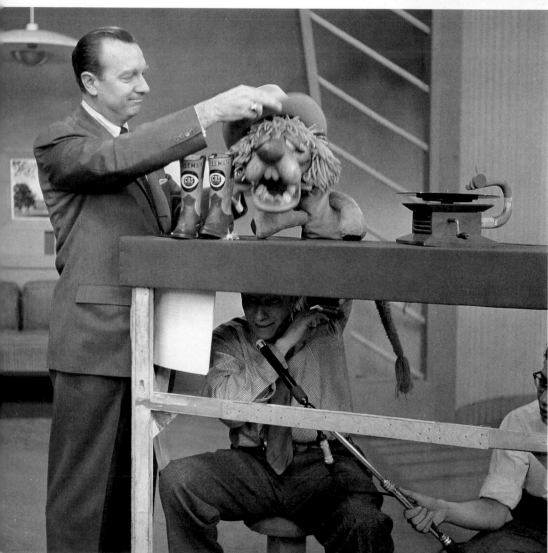

Two years after NBC launched *Today*, starring Dave Garroway and a chimp named J. Fred Muggs, CBS answered with *The Morning Show.* Its first host was newsman **Walter Cronkite**, whose duties included repartee with puppets manipulated by **Bil Baird** (under the table). Both Cronkite and Baird survived the experience.

GEORGE BURNS

and

GRACIE ALLEN

On playing their fourth medium (after vaudeville, movies, and radio):

George: "Gracie, what do you think of television?"

Gracie: "I think it's wonderful. I hardly watch radio anymore."

George: "Say good night, Gracie."

Gracie: "Good night, Gracie."

19**55**

The Soviet Union consolidates its grip on Eastern Europe by way of the Warsaw Pact, a military alliance with seven satellite nations. Argentina's military overthrows dictator Juan Perón, 60. Baseball's Dodgers win their only World Series while playing in Brooklyn.

Premiering series: *Alfred Hitchcock Presents* (CBS); *Captain Kangaroo* (CBS); *Cheyenne* (ABC); *Gunsmoke* (CBS); *The Honeymooners* (CBS); *The Lawrence Welk Show* (ABC); *The Mickey Mouse Club* (ABC); *The Millionaire* (CBS); *The $64,000 Question* (CBS); *You'll Never Get Rich* (CBS).

Movies: *Bad Day at Black Rock*; *Blackboard Jungle*; *Lady and the Tramp*; *Marty* (Oscar); *Rebel Without a Cause*.

Songs: "Cherry Pink and Apple Blossom White" (Perez Prado); "The Ballad of Davy Crockett" (Bill Hayes); "Rock Around the Clock" (Bill Haley and the Comets); "Unchained Melody" (Les Baxter).

Books: *Andersonville* (Mackinlay Kantor); *Gift from the Sea* (Anne Morrow Lindbergh); *Lolita* (Vladimir Nabokov); *The Trial* (Franz Kafka).

Died: actor James Dean, 24; physicist Albert Einstein, 76; biologist Alexander Fleming, discoverer of penicillin, 73; novelist Thomas Mann, 80; jazzman Charlie "Bird" Parker, 34; playwright Robert Sherwood, 59.

Debuts: coonskin caps (inspired by Disney's *Davy Crockett*); Ford Thunderbird; Play-Doh; advice columnist Ann Landers.

With an armistice in Korea, the U.S. Army was at peace again—and ripe for satire. In *You'll Never Get Rich* (later retitled *The Phil Silvers Show*), bespectacled **Phil Silvers** played the endlessly conniving Sergeant Bilko and rotund **Maurice Gosfeld** (at the star's right elbow) the sad-sack Private Doberman. In the show's first season, Silvers won both Best Actor and Best Comedian Emmys.

Spurred by the box-office hits *High Noon* and *Shane*, CBS tailored a televersion of its radio show *Gunsmoke* for John Wayne. The Duke said nope but suggested **James Arness**, 32, for the lead of TV's first adult Western. The 6'7" Arness played Marshall Dillon and **Dennis Weaver** (right) his first deputy, Chester. Dodge City would see enough guest gunslingers like **Charles Bronson** to run 20 seasons, 14 of them in Nielsen's Top 15 and four at No. 1.

The televersion of an old radio quiz show really upped the stakes: players entered a soundproof booth when **Hal March** posed *The $64,000 Question* (1,000 times radio's top prize). The series knocked *I Love Lucy* from atop the Nielsens as then-unknowns like Dr. Joyce Brothers, Barbara Feldon (later of *Get Smart*) and dancer Geoffrey Holder won big. Though never implicated in the game-fixing scandals, the show was abruptly axed in 1958.

Ford Star Jubilee's live adaptation of the play *High Tor* was noteworthy on two counts. First, the Maxwell Anderson drama was transformed into a musical, with the leads played by **Bing Crosby** and **Nancy Olson**. Second, the role of the friendly ghost was sung by a 20-year-old British performer making her U.S. TV debut: **Julie Andrews**.

45

On December 1, police in Montgomery, Alabama, jailed bus rider Rosa Parks, 42, for refusing to move to the blacks-only section at the back, as required by law. That didn't warrant national coverage. What happened four days later did: a black boycott of the city's buses, led by the Reverend Martin Luther King Jr., that would end 382 days later when the Supreme Court ruled the Montgomery ordinance unconstitutional.

In his movies, **Alfred Hitchcock** always engineered himself a sneaky cameo appearance. No need to on *Alfred Hitchcock Presents*; the British director personally introduced each of the anthology series' tales of mystery and suspense. During the show's 10-season run, on two networks, Hitchcock also directed an average of two episodes per year.

JACKIE GLEASON

On The Honey-mooners, *whose 39 filmed episodes ran in 1955–56:*

"I actually lived at Ralph's address, 358 Chauncey Street in Brooklyn. The set was my living room and kitchen as a kid. And all the Honey-mooners were right out of that building. I knew a thousand couples like these, the loudmouth hus-band with a wife a hell of a lot smarter. And every block had a crazy nut like Norton."

Eisenhower defeats Stevenson again to retain the presidency. Egypt's Gamal Abdel Nasser seizes the Suez Canal; when Britain, France, and Israel respond militarily, the U.S. and U.S.S.R. team to force a cease-fire. Moscow also bloodily suppresses a rebellion in Hungary. New York Yankee Don Larsen pitches the first (and still only) perfect World Series game. Actress Grace Kelly, 28, weds Prince Rainier III of Monaco, 33.

Premiering series: *As the World Turns* (CBS); *Edge of Night* (CBS); *Playhouse 90* (CBS); *The Steve Allen Show* (NBC); *The Tennessee Ernie Ford Show* (NBC); *Twenty-One* (NBC); *Zane Grey Theater* (CBS).

Movies: *Anastasia*; *Around the World in 80 Days* (Oscar); *The King and I*; Bergman's *The Seventh Seal*; *The Ten Commandments*.

Songs: "Don't Be Cruel"/"Hound Dog" (Elvis Presley); "The Great Pretender" (The Platters); "I Walk the Line" (Johnny Cash); "The Wayward Wind" (Gogi Grant); "Why Do Fools Fall in Love" (Frankie Lymon and the Teenagers).

Books: *The Organization Man* (W.H. Whyte); *Peyton Place* (Grace Metalious); *Profiles in Courage* (John F. Kennedy).

Died: frozen-food pioneer Clarence Birdseye, 69; playwright Bertolt Brecht, 58; artist Jackson Pollock, 44; *Winnie-the-Pooh* creator A.A. Milne, 75; athlete Babe Didrikson Zaharias, 42.

Debuts: Burger King; Comet cleanser.

Okay, it wasn't the phenom's first TV gig (which had come seven months earlier, on CBS's *Stage Show*). And with *The Ed Sullivan Show*'s host out ill, he was introduced by stand-in Charles Laughton. And he wasn't shot only from the waist up; that happened on his third visit. Still, September 9 lives on as the night America rocked as 22-year-old **Elvis Presley** sang "Don't Be Cruel," "Reddy Teddy," "Love Me Tender," and—natch— "Hound Dog."

Breaking the 15-minute-soap barrier, *As the World Turns* took a half hour to peel back the placid veneer of Oakdale (like, who knew **Ruth Warrick** and **Les Damon** were enjoying an adulterous fling?). Other regulars have included Tovah Feldshuh, Eileen Fulton, Farley Granger, Parker Posey, Meg Ryan, Richard Thomas, and Robert Vaughn.

While the Suez Canal crisis transfixed the world, Poland and Hungary were edging toward the brink of bolting the Soviet empire. On November 2, Moscow rolled 16 divisions and 2,000 tanks into Hungary. Armed Freedom Fighters took to the streets and even captured tanks, but their resistance was crushed in two days.

April 14, 1865. Evening. Abraham Lincoln (**Raymond Massey**) and wife Mary (**Lillian Gish**) settle into their box at Ford's Theater in Washington, D.C. In stalks John Wilkes Booth (**Jack Lemmon**, three days after his 31st birthday). The live drama *The Day Lincoln Was Shot* recreated the American tragedy on *Ford Star Jubilee*.

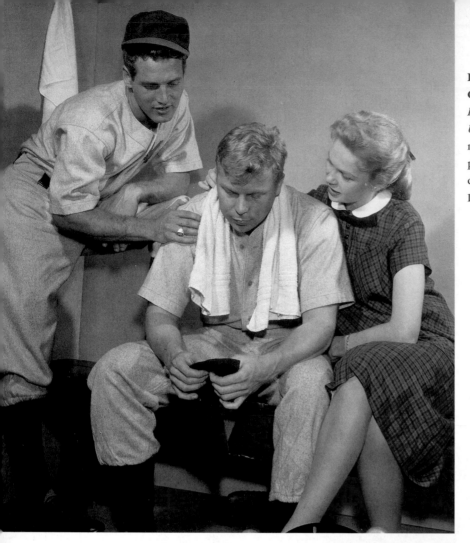

Paul Newman (left), **Albert Salmi**, and **Georgeanne Johnson** were principals in *Bang the Drum Slowly*, a live drama on *The U.S. Steel Hour* adapted from the Mark Harris novel. The tale of a big league catcher who plays one last season while battling a fatal disease was also filmed in 1973 with Robert DeNiro and Michael Moriarty.

Playhouse 90 had a heady launch. Its second live production, *Requiem for a Heavyweight*, won Emmys for Best Single Program; best script (Rod Serling); Best Direction (Ralph Nelson), and Best Single Performance (**Jack Palance**, here flanked by **Ed Wynn** [right] and son **Keenan Wynn**). In the 1962 movie version, their roles were played by Anthony Quinn, Mickey Rooney, and Jackie Gleason, and one featured extra was the young boxer Cassius Clay.

• • • • • • • • •

BOB KEESHAN

Twenty-nine, on the credo that would win Captain Kangaroo *30 years on-air and four Emmys:*

"A respect for children, their intelligence, their potential good taste. I think civility and good manners are very important in society."

The U.S.S.R. orbits *Sputniks I* and *II* (the latter carries pooch Laika into space one-way). Federal troops prevent Arkansas Governor Orval Faubus from blocking integration of Little Rock's Central High School. Black tennis player Althea Gibson, 29, wins both the Wimbledon and U.S. Open titles.

Premiering series: *American Bandstand* (ABC); *Have Gun, Will Travel* (CBS); *Leave It to Beaver* (CBS); *Maverick* (ABC); *Perry Mason* (CBS); *The Real McCoys* (ABC); *Richard Diamond, Private Detective* (CBS); *Sea Hunt* (SYND); *Sugarfoot* (ABC); *Wagon Train* (NBC).

Movies: Vadim's *And God Created Woman* (with Brigitte Bardot); *The Bridge on the River Kwai* (Oscar); *A Face in the Crowd*; *Old Yeller*; *The Three Faces of Eve.*

Songs: "Banana Boat (Day-O)" (Harry Belafonte); "Chances Are" (Johnny Mathis); "Little Darlin'" (The Diamonds); "Peggy Sue" (Buddy Holly); "Wake Up, Little Susie" (The Everly Brothers).

Books: *Atlas Shrugged* (Ayn Rand); *The Cat in the Hat* (Dr. Seuss); *On the Beach* (Nevil Shute); *On the Road* (Jack Kerouac).

Died: actor Humphrey Bogart, 57; polar explorer Richard Byrd, 68; designer Christian Dior, 52; muralist Diego Rivera, 70; conductor Arturo Toscanini, 90.

Debuts: a scale to measure earthquake severity (devised by seismologist Charles Richter); Wham-O's Pluto Platter (later renamed the Frisbee); Ford Edsel.

In a documentary notable for its prescience, CBS News traveled to Cuba to profile a fledgling guerrilla movement aiming to oust dictator Fulgencio Batista. Highlight of *The Rebels of Sierra Madre:* a talk with the rebel commandante, a one-time minor-league pitcher for the Washington Senators, 30-year old **Fidel Castro**.

"A knight without armor in a savage land" was how *Have Gun Will Travel*'s theme song described its hero. The mercenary played by **Richard Boone** had a college diploma, a taste for gourmet food and wine, a lightning draw—and even the most unique first name in TV history. It said so right on his calling card: "Wire Paladin/San Francisco."

A little soft shoe was to be expected on *The Danny Thomas Show,* since its star portrayed a nightclub entertainer. Having originated four years earlier on ABC under the title *Make Room for Daddy,* the sitcom moved to CBS, where it would run another seven seasons. **Rusty Hamer** (left) and couchbound **Ben Lessy** were from the ABC cast; **Marjorie Lord** and young **Angela Cartwright** joined the CBS version.

A quarter-century after his creation by mystery writer Erle Stanley Gardner, and following a lengthy stint on radio, *Perry Mason* hung out his shingle on TV. **Raymond Burr** was an unlikely casting choice; when not playing heavies (*Rear Window*), he had made B-movies (the original *Godzilla*). But over the next nine years, his sympathetic defense attorney would spring— no joke—271 consecutive clients.

After two years of negotiations led by CBS President Frank Stanton, **Nikita Khrushchev** agreed to be filmed in the Kremlin, unrehearsed, for an edition of *Face the Nation.* Though the Soviet premier arrived late, refused makeup, and appeared testy at some of the questions, the *New York Times* called the show "the season's most extraordinary hour of broadcasting."

Composers **Richard Rodgers** and **Oscar Hammerstein** sat in as **Julie Andrews** rehearsed their original musical version of *Cinderella*. The 90-minute primetime special, broadcast on March 31, drew what was then the largest television audience ever.

Haircuts that went awry were a typical plot-line on *Leave It to Beaver*, a sitcom starring **Jerry Mathers**, 9, as Theodore (Beaver) Cleaver and **Tony Dow**, 12, as brother Wally. Never a Top 20 hit during its six seasons on two networks, the reruns were to attain cult status (as witness the erroneous rumors that Mathers had died in Vietnam).

● ● ● ● ● ● ● ● ●

PHIL SILVERS

On his signature role as an Army sergeant-cum-scam artist:

"Nat [Hiken, series creator] named him after Steve Bilko, a minor league player who had hit 61 homers. I didn't have time to learn military commands, but I figured the audience would know that when I bark it's a command, even if the bark's unrecognizable as any particular word. One writer tried to spell it. The closest he could come was 'Ha-yarp!'"

rance, torn over the issue of Algerian independence, asks World War II hero Charles de Gaulle, 69, to form a government. The Baltimore Colts win the NFL title by beating the New York Giants, 23–17, in pro football's first sudden-death overtime. Brazil captures soccer's World Cup behind 17-year-old Edson Arantes do Nascimento (aka Pelé).

Premiering series: *Bat Masterson* (NBC); *The Donna Reed Show* (ABC); *The Garry Moore Show* (CBS); *Naked City* (ABC); *Peter Gunn* (NBC); *The Rifleman* (ABC); *77 Sunset Strip* (ABC); *Wanted: Dead or Alive* (CBS).

Movies: *The Defiant Ones*; *Gigi* (Oscar); *South Pacific*; Tati's *Mon Oncle*; *Vertigo*.

Songs: "At the Hop" (Danny and the Juniors); "Great Balls of Fire" (Jerry Lee Lewis); "Nel Blu Dipinto di Blu (Volare)" (Domenico Modugno): "Patricia" (Perez Prado); "Tequila" (The Champs); "Tom Dooley" (The Kingston Trio).

Books: *The Affluent Society* (John Kenneth Galbraith); *Breakfast at Tiffany's* (Truman Capote); *Doctor Zhivago* (Boris Pasternak, who declines the Nobel Prize).

Died: blues composer W.C. Handy, 84; photographer Edward Weston, 72.

Debuts: major league baseball in California (Opening Day: Los Angeles Dodgers vs. San Francisco Giants); the Grammy Awards; Sweet 'n Low; Pizza Hut; Bic disposable pen; Hula Hoops; Mr. Clean cleanser; the John Birch Society.

Had **Garry Moore** (left) been a contestant on his first primetime hit (*I've Got a Secret*, a Top 10 fixture since 1955), the correct answer would've been: As of September, he also began hosting a variety series. Among the regulars on *The Garry Moore Show* were **Carol Burnett** and **Durward Kirby**.

America was caught off-guard when the Soviets won the race into space by launching *Sputnik I* on October 4, 1957. As Congress scrambled to create and fund NASA, the U.S. Army put a satellite into orbit on its second try, on January 31. Explaining *Explorer I*'s technology was **Walter Cronkite** (who would anchor CBS coverage of America's space missions into the 1980s).

Old hoofers never die, they just waltz away…Two nights after 47-year-old **Ginger Rogers** tripped the light fantastic in her own primetime CBS special, her partner in nine Hollywood musicals, 59-year-old Fred Astaire, headlined his own special on NBC.

In February **Leonard Bernstein**, 40, the new director of the New York Philharmonic Orchestra, conducted a *Young People's Concert* to demystify classical music. The special was sufficiently popular that later in the year he and the orchestra performed an encore, this time for grown-ups.

At 28, **Steve McQueen** segued from B-movies like *The Blob* and *Never Trust a Stranger* (opposite Drew Barrymore's dad, John Jr.) into his first primetime series. Packing a sawed-off carbine, he scoured the Old West for desperadoes who were *Wanted: Dead or Alive*. McQueen spent his first summer hiatus filming a movie whose 1960 release would enable him to resume his big-screen career: *The Magnificent Seven*.

● ● ● ● ● ● ● ● ● ●

JAMES ARNESS

On his Gunsmoke *character as the show began its second (of four) years as TV's No. 1 show:*

"Dillon is a pathetic and tragic figure. All these guys were. They had nothing. They were all a bit tilted, sadists even—they liked to hurt people. They died in the most ignominious ways. That's what makes Dillon interesting."

irst man-made object on the moon: the Soviet *Lunik 2*, which crash-lands on the "near" side; *Lunik 3* beams back first pictures of the "dark" side. Fidel Castro, 32, achieves power in Cuba. The Dalai Lama, 24, flees Chinese-controlled Tibet for India. TV sets in use: 50 million.

Premiering series: *Bonanza* (NBC); *Dennis the Menace* (CBS); *G.E. College Bowl* (CBS); *Hawaiian Eye* (ABC); *The Many Loves of Dobie Gillis* (CBS); *Mr. Lucky* (CBS); *Rawhide* (CBS); *The Twilight Zone* (CBS); *The Untouchables* (ABC).

Movies: *Anatomy of a Murder*; *Ben-Hur* (Oscar); Camus's *Black Orpheus*; Godard's *Breathless*; *Some Like It Hot*.

Songs: "Mack the Knife" (Bobby Darin); "Mr. Blue" (The Fleetwoods); "Stagger Lee" (Lloyd Price); "A Teenager in Love" (Dion and the Belmonts); "What'd I Say" (Ray Charles).

Books: *Exodus* (Leon Uris); *Hawaii* (James Michener); *The Longest Day* (Cornelius Ryan); *The Tin Drum* (Günter Grass).

Died: novelist Raymond Chandler, 70; director Cecil B. DeMille, 78; singer Billie Holiday, 44; rockers Buddy Holly, 22, and Ritchie Valens, 17 (in a plane crash in Iowa); architect Frank Lloyd Wright, 89.

Debuts: the integrated circuit, or microchip (invented by Robert Noyce and Jack Kilby); Barbie doll; Tamla Records (later renamed Motown by founder Berry Gordy Jr.).

Formula for a hit—transform *Wagon Train*'s settlers into cattle and cast as the leads two struggling actors: **Clint Eastwood**, 29 (left, of *Francis in the Navy*, starring a talking mule), and **Eric Fleming**, 35 (of *Queen of Outer Space*, starring Zsa Zsa Gabor). Eastwood would stay on *Rawhide* even after his 1964 breakthrough spaghetti Western, *A Fistful of Dollars*. Fleming would quit in 1965 and drown the next year in Peru while filming another B-movie.

Was it Love Potion No. 9 that Zelda (**Sheila James**) was preparing for Dobie (**Dwayne Hickman**, center)? Whatever, Maynard G. Krebs (**Bob Denver**) was, like, digging it. Zelda's schemes to snare her guy never worked during the four-season run of *The Many Loves of Dobie Gillis* (early regulars: Warren Beatty and Tuesday Weld). But the couple would be man and wife by 1977, when a reunion telemovie aired.

When the 90-minute variety series *The Big Party* didn't come close to living up to its name, ratings-wise, CBS filled two-thirds of the time slot with *The Revlon Revue*. The hour built around **Harry Belafonte** earned the 32-year-old singer an Emmy.

Six weeks past her 13th birthday, **Liza Minnelli** partnered 46-year-old **Gene Kelly** on a primetime special hosted by the dancer. Another guest: the poet Carl Sandburg, who preferred to spin words rather than around the stage.

Fifty stars graced the American flag for the first time on August 21 when Hawaii entered the Union. After signing the legislation, President **Dwight Eisenhower** helped unfurl the new design, the 20th in the history of the Republic. (No. 19, with 49 stars, had been introduced just eight-and-a-half months earlier, on Alaska's statehood.)

The NCAA basketball tournament was still a yawner (only two dozen schools were invited to compete each March) when **Allen Ludden** launched *G.E. College Bowl.* Each Sunday afternoon, teams of undergraduates matched brains in hopes of winning money for their institution's scholarship fund.

ARLENE HIRST   LINDA LEE   R. WARREN

SMITH

TWILIGHT ZONE

"*Twilight Zone* will often fall on its duff and on occasion mistake pretension for maturity. But we haven't even scraped the surface of ideas. This is possibly the one anthology format that is not self-limiting—we can travel as high or as deep as the human imagination."

John F. Kennedy defeats Richard M. Nixon for the presidency. A U-2 spy plane flown by Francis Gary Powers, 30, is shot down over Russia. "Sit-ins" to integrate whites-only lunch counters start in Greensboro, North Carolina. Fifteen African colonies gain independence from Europe, including the Congo (now Zaire) and Nigeria. In Rome, heavyweight boxer Cassius Clay (later Muhammad Ali), 18, wins Olympic gold.

Premiering series: *The Andy Griffith Show* (CBS); *Candid Camera* (CBS); *The Flintstones* (ABC); *My Three Sons* (ABC); *Route 66* (CBS).

Movies: *The Apartment* (Oscar); Fellini's *La Dolce Vita*; *Elmer Gantry*; Dassin's *Never on Sunday*; *Psycho*; *Spartacus*.

Songs: "Chain Gang" (Sam Cooke); "El Paso" (Marty Robbins); "I'm Sorry" (Brenda Lee); "Save the Last Dance for Me" (The Drifters); "Theme from *A Summer Place*" (Percy Faith); "The Twist" (Chubby Checker).

Books: *Rabbit, Run* (John Updike); *The Rise and Fall of the Third Reich* (William Shirer); *To Kill a Mockingbird* (Harper Lee).

Died: writer Albert Camus, 47; actor Clark Gable, 59; novelist Boris Pasternak, 70; director Mack Sennett, 80.

Debuts: OPEC, founded by Iran, Iraq, Kuwait, Saudi Arabia, and Venezuela; oral contraceptive; cardiac pacemaker; felt-tipped pen; the eight-team American Football League; the NFL Dallas Cowboys.

In 1858, while seeking a U.S. Senate seat from Illinois, Abraham Lincoln and Stephen Douglas engaged in an epic series of debates. One hundred two years later, White House candidates **John F. Kennedy** and **Richard M. Nixon** appeared in this and three later face-to-face clashes that were aired nationally on television and on radio. (In both elections, the Democrats would emerge victorious.)

Seven years before CBS newsman Charles Kuralt first went *On the Road*, a Yalie with a gleaming new Corvette (**Martin Milner**, at the wheel) and his blue collar buddy (**George Maharis**) began traversing America along *Route 66*. The series, filmed on location, often featured actors who would soon outgrow guest appearances, among them Robert Redford and Alan Alda.

In an edition of *CBS Reports* titled *Harvest of Shame*, Edward R. Murrow documented the stomach-turning callousness with which some U.S. agriculture giants treated their migrant farmworkers. In response to the show, which named names, one major beverage company threatened to pull its advertising from the network.

Not much happened in Mayberry. Certainly not crime, which left **Andy Griffith**'s widower sheriff ample time to teach son Opie (**Ronny Howard**, 6) lessons in life. Before the last "Gone Fishin'" sign was posted, *The Andy Griffith Show* would whistle through 249 episodes just as slow and easy as a summer afternoon in North Carolina.

At 34, **Richard Burton** was still little-known on this side of the Atlantic when he appeared with **Sally Ann Howe** in an adaptation of Ernest Hemingway's *The Fifth Column.* But by year's end the Welsh actor would star in the Broadway hit, *Camelot.* Next he would travel to Europe to film *The Longest Day* and then, on the set of *Cleopatra,* meet wife-to-be Elizabeth Taylor.

She came, she sprinted, she conquered. At the Summer Games in Rome **Wilma Rudolph**, 20, struck gold in the 100- and 200-meters and the 4-by-100 relay. Other Olympic heroes from CBS's 18-day coverage: U.S. decathlete Rafer Johnson and Ethiopian marathoner Abebe Bikila.

● ● ● ● ● ● ● ● ●

EILEEN
FULTON

*Shown at age 27,
on the character
she joined* As the
World Turns *to
portray (Lisa Miller,
soapdom's most
durable villainess):*

"I had not the
foggiest idea when
the bitch was born
that she would be
around for so
many years. Lisa is
a liar and a
schemer. I don't
think I'd enjoy
having her in my
house."

Soviet cosmonaut Yuri Gagarin, 27, is the first human in space. East Germany erects the Berlin Wall to keep its citizens from fleeing. Cuban expatriates seeking to overthrow Fidel Castro are defeated at the Bay of Pigs. Ex-Nazi Adolf Eichmann, kidnaped in Argentina by Israelis, is convicted of World War II crimes against Jews. New York Yankee outfielder Roger Maris's 61st home run breaks Babe Ruth's single-season record.

Premiering series: *The Alvin Show* (CBS); *Ben Casey* (ABC); *Car 54, Where Are You?* (NBC); *The Defenders* (CBS); *The Dick Van Dyke Show* (CBS); *Dr. Kildare* (NBC); *Mister Ed* (CBS).

Movies: *The Guns of Navarone*; *The Hustler*; Truffaut's *Jules and Jim*; *101 Dalmatians*; *West Side Story* (Oscar).

Songs: "Moon River" (Henry Mancini); "Quarter to Three" (Gary "U.S." Bonds); "Runaway" (Del Shannon); "Running Scared" (Roy Orbison); "Spanish Harlem" (Ben E. King); "Will You Love Me Tomorrow?" (The Shirelles).

Books: *Catch-22* (Joseph Heller); *The Making of the President: 1960* (Theodore White); *Silent Spring* (Rachel Carson).

Died: baseball's Ty Cobb, 74; actor Gary Cooper, 60; writer Ernest Hemingway, 61; psychiatrist Carl Jung, 85; humorist James Thurber, 66.

Debuts: the Peace Corps; in-flight movies (courtesy of TWA); Pampers; Sprite.

Fifteen minutes after liftoff from Cape Canaveral, astronaut **Alan Shepard**, 37, splashed down in the Atlantic off the Bahamas and stepped from *Freedom 7* onto the carrier *Lake Champlain*. Having just flown to an altitude of 115 miles, he was the first American to reach space and the second human (33 days behind Yuri Gagarin, who also orbited Earth once).

Upon leaving the White House, **Dwight Eisenhower** granted **Walter Cronkite** a series of exclusive interviews that aired in three hour-long *CBS Reports*. In one, subject and interviewer visited a windswept cemetery in Normandy. It was the final resting place for many Allied soldiers who on June 6, 1944—D Day—had waded ashore, under then-General Eisenhower's orders, to begin liberating France from Adolf Hitler's army.

Unlike Perry Mason, the father-and-son legal team who were *The Defenders* tackled timely cases involving abortion, civil disobedience and mercy killing—and sometimes lost. The show won four Emmys its first season, including best dramatic program. Also honored, as best actor: **E.G. Marshall** (left, with costar **Robert Reed**, right). Guest star **William Shatner** played Reed's role in the 1957 *Studio One* production from which the hour-long series was drawn.

One singer who never had to tell the brass section to pipe down was **Ethel Merman**. The Broadway star joined Frank Sinatra and Maurice Chevalier to headline *The Gershwin Years*, a primetime special celebrating the works of two boys from Brooklyn, composer George and his lyricist brother Ira.

What if they put on a sitcom about gag writers and nobody laughed? Few did during *The Dick Van Dyke Show*'s first season, which was spent in Nielsen's basement. But critical praise, a kinder time slot—and an effervescent cast led by **Dick Van Dyke**, 35, and **Mary Tyler Moore**, 23—would spark a rebound. In its second year, the series cracked the Top 10 and won three Emmys, including one for best comedy.

Didn't anyone tell *Mister Ed* that baseballs are upholstered in horsehide? The sitcom's second banana, Alan Young, was probably too abashed, and he was the only human with whom the equine would converse (with help from gravel-voiced character actor Rocky Lane). So why was the palomino chasing fastballs? Maybe to impress a Phillie?

THOSE
WONDERFUL
YEARS

• • • • • • • • • •

GARRY MOORE

On hosting the series that captured an Emmy for Outstanding Program in the Field of Variety:

"Fred Allen called fellows like Ed Sullivan, Jack Paar, and me 'pointers.' He meant that we simply introduce performers with real talent, then get off the stage while they enter-tain the people. He said a dog could be taught the same trick by smearing meat on the actors."

The Cuban Missile Crisis ends with President Kennedy forcing Khrushchev to withdraw Soviet missiles and fighter jets from Castro's Caribbean nation. John Glenn, 40, is the first American to orbit Earth. Algeria gains its independence from France. South Africa jails anti-apartheid activist Nelson Mandela, 44. Wilt Chamberlain sets an NBA one-game record by scoring 100 points against the Knicks.

Premiering series: *The Beverly Hillbillies* (CBS); *McHale's Navy* (ABC); *The Virginian* (NBC).

Movies: *Birdman of Alcatraz*; *Dr. No*; *Lawrence of Arabia* (Oscar); *The Longest Day*; *The Manchurian Candidate*.

Songs: "Big Girls Don't Cry" (The Four Seasons); "Duke of Earl" (Gene Chandler); "I Left My Heart in San Francisco" (Tony Bennett); "Peppermint Twist" (Joey Dee and the Starliters); "Surfin' Safari" (The Beach Boys).

Books: *The Gutenberg Galaxy* (Marshall McLuhan); *One Flew Over the Cuckoo's Nest* (Ken Kesey); *Silent Spring* (Rachel Carson).

Died: physicist Neils Bohr, 77; poet e.e. cummings, 67; novelist William Faulkner, 64; comedian Ernie Kovacs, 42; actress Marilyn Monroe, 36; Eleanor Roosevelt, 78.

Debuts: baseball's Houston Colt .45s (later renamed the Astros) and New York Mets; as host of *The Tonight Show*, Johnny Carson, 37.

Forget the grapes of wrath—in *The Beverly Hillbillies*, that clan wheezing into 90210 was the oil-rich Clampetts, late of the Ozarks. (Why ain't there no steer ropers on Rodeo Drive, Jed?) The sitcom immediately soared atop the Nielsens, where it remained for two seasons. Its stars: **Buddy Ebsen** (riding shotgun); **Max Baer Jr.**; **Irene Ryan** as Granny, and **Donna Douglas**.

Flanked by U.S. marshals and backed by federal writs, 29-year-old **James Meredith** became the first known black student at the University of Mississippi. He had been accepted the previous year, but Governor Ross Barnett used state troopers to bar his entrance. Four years later, Meredith would be shot while working to register black voters.

After enduring 10 weather-related delays, **John Glenn**, 40, finally strode to the launchpad at Cape Canaveral. Minutes later the astronaut became the first American (and third human) to orbit Earth. Glenn's three-orbit, 2-hour-56-minute mission prompted President Kennedy to call for landing an American on the moon by decade's end.

At 32, First Lady **Jacqueline Bouvier
Kennedy** guided viewers through the
newly refurbished First House at 1600
Pennsylvania Avenue in Washington, D.C.

CBS News produced *A Tour of the White
House with Mrs. John F. Kennedy*, which
aired on two networks.

Was it that high-kicking *kazatsky*, or Cossack dance, performed by **Julie Andrews** and **Carol Burnett** that goaded Nikita Khrushchev into arming Cuba with Soviet missiles? Whatever, Burnett won an Emmy for the musical comedy special, as did the show itself, *Julie and Carol at Carnegie Hall.*

Judy Garland warmed up for her impending primetime series by way of a special featuring pals **Dean Martin** and **Frank Sinatra**. The ratings for this outing were far kinder than for 1963's *The Judy Garland Show*, which would have the misfortune of being scheduled directly opposite *Bonanza*.

In
Their
Own
Words

• • • • • • • • • •

Douglas Edwards

First CBS News anchor, on handing over his duties, after 15 years, to Walter Cronkite:

"It is my contention that radio and TV have helped democratize this country. We have submitted to the scrutiny of the camera's powerful eye, and the microphone's searching ear, the backwoods and the backrooms, and they'll never be the same again."

1963

Two days after he is charged with assassinating President Kennedy, ex-Marine Lee Harvey Oswald, 24, is shot dead while in police custody by Dallas nightclub owner Jack Ruby. First woman in space: Soviet cosmonaut Valentina Tereshkova, 26. In Britain, the team that perpetrates "The Great Train Robbery" makes off with $7 million.

Premiering series: *Burke's Law* (ABC); *East Side, West Side* (CBS); *The Fugitive* (ABC); *General Hospital* (ABC); *The Judy Garland Show* (CBS); *Let's Make a Deal* (NBC); *My Favorite Martian* (CBS); *The Outer Limits* (ABC); *Petticoat Junction* (CBS).

Movies: *Cleopatra*; Fellini's *8½*; *The Great Escape*; *Hud*; *Tom Jones* (Oscar).

Songs: "Blowin' in the Wind" (Bob Dylan); "Danke Schoen" (Wayne Newton); "Fingertips—Part II" (Little Stevie Wonder); "Louie Louie" (The Kingsmen); "Puff the Magic Dragon" (Peter, Paul and Mary); "Surf City" (Jan and Dean).

Books: *The Feminine Mystique* (Betty Friedan); *The Fire Next Time* (James Baldwin); *V* (Thomas Pynchon); *Where the Wild Things Are* (Maurice Sendak).

Died: artist-writer Jean Cocteau, 74; black intellectual W.E.B. Du Bois, 95; poet Robert Frost, 88; Pope John XXIII, 82; poet Sylvia Plath, 31 (by suicide).

Debuts: state lottery (in New Hampshire); metal tennis racket (invented by Rene Lacoste); Valium; Weight Watchers.

At 1:40 P.M. Eastern Standard Time on Friday, November 22, CBS News scooped the other networks by interrupting *As the World Turns* with a startling bulletin: while on a political trip to Dallas, **John F. Kennedy** had been shot. A short while later **Walter Cronkite** confirmed to the nation that the president was dead. For the next 55 hours CBS would preempt regularly scheduled programming to cover the Kennedy funeral and the transition of power to Lyndon B. Johnson.

"I have a dream," declared **Martin Luther King Jr.**, 34, on August 28 in the eloquent speech on racial equality that would become his signature. His immediate audience was some 200,000 supporters of a pending civil rights bill who had marched on Washington. The rally was also broadcast nationally; CBS News's report included five hours of live coverage.

Few series were more ambitious than *East Side/West Side* in dramatizing the chasms in American society. **George C. Scott**, 35, starred as a New York City social worker and Cicely Tyson portrayed his secretary. The show's focus on issues like drug addiction, welfare, and slumlords won critical praise but lackluster Nielsens.

Making a rare appearance on American television, **Ingrid Bergman**, 48, played the achingly modern heroine of Henrik Ibsen's 1890 play, *Hedda Gabler.* Her supporting cast in the 90-minute production, which was taped in London: **Trevor Howard**, Michael Redgrave, and Ralph Richardson.

E.T. he wasn't (nor, for that matter, an Orkian named Mork). But **Ray Walston** (right) became *My Favorite Martian* when he left the fourth rock from the Sun and crash-landed in Los Angeles. Reporter **Bill Bixby** took in "Uncle Martin" while the alien tried to repair his spaceship, a feat that escaped him for three years and 107 episodes.

Not much was alive with the sound of music when **Danny Kaye** and guest **Imogene Coca** teamed tonsils in a skit from *The Danny Kaye Show*. In his first season on television, the veteran funnyman won an Emmy for best variety performer and his show another for best variety program.

● ● ● ● ● ● ● ● ●

RED SKELTON

*Whose series
finished the
season at No. 3
in the Nielsens,
on his craft:*

"The idea in
comedy is to start
out, get in trouble,
and get out of it.
I just want to be
known as a clown
because to me,
that's the height
of my profession.
It means you can
do everything—
sing, dance, and,
above all, make
people laugh."

Lyndon B. Johnson defeats Barry Goldwater for the presidency. Congress authorizes military action against North Vietnam via the Tonkin Gulf Resolution. Nikita Khrushchev, 70, loses Kremlin power to Leonid Brezhnev, 57. Haiti's François Duvalier, 57, proclaims himself president-for-life. Police capture "Boston Strangler" Albert DeSalvo, 32.

Premiering series: *Bewitched* (ABC); *Gilligan's Island* (CBS); *Gomer Pyle, U.S.M.C.* (CBS); *The Man from U.N.C.L.E.* (NBC); *The Munsters* (CBS); *Peyton Place* (ABC).

Movies: *Dr. Strangelove*; *A Hard Day's Night*; *Mary Poppins*; *My Fair Lady* (Oscar); Cacoyannis's *Zorba the Greek*.

Songs: "Baby Love" (The Supremes); "The Girl from Ipanema" (Stan Getz and Astrud Gilberto); "Hello, Dolly!" (Louis Armstrong); "I Want to Hold Your Hand" (The Beatles); "My Guy" (Mary Wells).

Books: *Harriet the Spy* (Louise Fitzhugh); *Herzog* (Saul Bellow); *Smoking and Health* (Surgeon General Luther Terry's report warning of diseases associated with cigarette smoking).

Died: President Herbert Hoover, 90; Indian prime minister Jawaharlal Nehru, 74; writer Flannery O'Connor, 39; composer Cole Porter, 72.

Debuts: the Washington, D.C., Beltway; Japan's *shinkansen*, or "bullet train;" Ford Mustang; zip codes; Pop-Tarts; topless swimsuit (by Rudi Gernreich).

The lyrics to their chart-topping hit "I Want to Hold Your Hand" were inaudible over the screaming teenyboppers packing the audience. No matter. In their U.S. debut, the Fab Four—**Paul**, 21; **Ringo**, 23; **George**, 20, and **John**, 23—brought Beatlemania to this side of the Pond. And coaxed a rare smile from the host of *The Ed Sullivan Show.*

The premise of *Gilligan's Island* was pure
Agatha Christie—strand seven people on a
desert island. The execution was pure farce,
thanks to a cast that included (from left) **Jim
Backus**; **Russell Johnson**; **Natalie Schafer**;
Bob Denver as Gilligan; **Tina Louise**; **Alan
Hale Jr.**; and **Dawn Wells**.

In hopes it would help "eliminate the last vestiges of injustice in America," President **Lyndon Johnson** signed the Civil Rights Act of 1964. The bill outlawed racially motivated discrimination in areas from employment to union membership to public accommodations. Various courts would later broaden the scope of the landmark legislation.

Now it can be revealed: during a life that began in the Dark Ages, Grandpa Munster (**Al Lewis**) found time to invent the gravity boot. Heading the family that lived at 1313 Mockingbird Lane, home of *The Munsters*, were **Yvonne DeCarlo** and **Fred Gwynne**.

CBS, like all the networks, derived substantial advertising revenues from tobacco companies. Yet after U.S. Surgeon General Luther Terry officially linked cigarette smoking to lung cancer, emphysema, and heart diseases, CBS explored the risks in a primetime documentary hosted by **Harry Reasoner**.

America was still at peace when **Jim Nabors** took the character he had created on *The Andy Griffith Show* and made him a Leatherneck (much to the rue of top kick **Frank Sutton**). During *Gomer Pyle, U.S.M.C.*'s five-year run, the sitcom would remain untouched by the events in Vietnam.

● ● ● ● ● ● ● ●

DICK VAN DYKE

Winner of his second straight acting Emmy, on his comedic roots:

"As a kid, I spent my Saturdays watching Laurel and Hardy. Nobody ever accused me of stealing from Stan Laurel—except he recognized it when I finally met him in his later years."

1965

American warplanes bomb North Vietnam. President Johnson doubles the draft to increase the number of U.S. troops in South Vietnam to 125,000. Ferdinand Marcos, 48, is elected president of the Philippines. Los Angeles's Watts district is hit by race riots. Nine Northeastern states and southeastern Canada are hit by the Great Blackout.

Premiering series: *The Big Valley* (ABC); *The F.B.I.* (ABC); *Get Smart* (NBC); *Green Acres* (CBS); *Hogan's Heroes* (CBS); *I Dream of Jeannie* (NBC); *I Spy* (NBC); *Lost in Space* (CBS); *Run for Your Life* (NBC); *The Wild, Wild West* (CBS). .

Movies: Pontecorvo's *The Battle of Algiers*; *Cat Ballou*; *Darling*; *The Pawnbroker*; *The Sound of Music* (Oscar).

Songs: "Downtown" (Petula Clark); "I Got You, Babe" (Sonny and Cher); "(I Can't Get No) Satisfaction" (The Rolling Stones); "King of the Road" (Roger Miller); "My Girl" (The Temptations); "Wooly Bully" (Sam the Sham and the Pharaohs).

Books: *The Autobiography of Malcolm X* (with Alex Haley); *In Cold Blood* (Truman Capote); *Unsafe at Any Speed* (Ralph Nader).

Died: British statesman Winston Churchill, 90; singer Nat "King" Cole, 45; journalist Edward R. Murrow, 56; cosmetics czar Helena Rubenstein, 94; Malcolm X, 40 (by assassination).

Debuts: Medicare; all-news radio (New York's WINS); Kevlar; miniskirt.

Good-bye rat race, hello 4-H contests. In a reversal on *The Beverly Hillbillies*, a midtown lawyer (**Eddie Albert**) and his uptown wife (**Eva Gabor**) quit New York for rustic Hooterville, where instead of sirens they could hear things that went *baaaa* in the night. *Green Acres*'s gentle barnyard humor played well; the sitcom climbed as high as No. 6 in the Nielsens during its six-year run.

The 1953 movie *Stalag 17* played life in a World War II POW camp as black comedy. *Hogan's Heroes* played it as slapstick; despite the efforts of Nazi nitwits like **John Banner**, eponymous top banana **Bob Crane** (left) always had the last say. (Five years after the sitcom ended, cast member Richard Dawson would go on to game-show stardom by hosting *Family Feud*.)

En route in 1997 to Alpha Centauri, seven Earthlings got themselves *Lost in Space*. The cast (from left): Robot (Bob May, voice by Dick Tufeld); **June Lockhart**; **Guy Williams** (TV's original *Zorro*); **Marta Kristen**; **Mark Goddard**; **Billy Mumy**; **Jonathan Harris**, and **Angela Cartwright**. The 1998 movie reviving this Family Robinson (Americans by birth, not Swiss) would star William Hurt.

A holiday classic was born with the premiere of *A Charlie Brown Christmas*, the first prime-time special drawn from Charles Schulz's *Peanuts* strip. Adding to the Emmy-winning program's charm was its whimsical score, by the jazz composer and pianist Vince Guaraldi.

Fresh from conquering Broadway in the
musical *Funny Girl*, a petite Brooklyn native
with an outsized vocal reach (and a quirky
sense of spelling) went national with her
own primetime special. *My Name Is Barbra*,
airing four days after its star turned 23,
earned two Emmys: best show and best indi-
vidual achievement, by **Barbra Streisand**.

The tinder: poverty and despair, long
watchwords in the Watts district of
Los Angeles. The spark: rumors that
police had brutalized a local man
stopped for drunk driving. The result:
a five-day rampage that required
20,000 National Guards to quell.
Thirty-plus died, hundreds were
injured, and 4,000 arrested. The physical scars inflicted on the predomi-
nantly black neighborhood would
remain unhealed a generation later.

MORLEY SAFER

Whose report showing a Marine igniting a Vietnamese hut with his Zippo lighter inflamed Washington, on media responsibility:

"A government official once said to me, 'Television has a built-in anti-war bias.' And I said, 'What should it have, a pro-war bias?'"

Mao Tse-tung orders a "Cultural Revolution" that plunges China into chaos for three years. Indira Gandhi, 46, is India's first woman prime minister. First black elected to the U.S. Senate in the 20th century: Edward Brooke, 47, of Massachusetts. First black to coach a major pro team: Bill Russell, 32, who also continues to play center for the Boston Celtics.

Premiering series: *The Avengers* (ABC); *Batman* (ABC); *Family Affair* (CBS); *Mission: Impossible* (CBS); *The Monkees* (NBC); *The Rat Patrol* (ABC); *Space Ghost* (CBS); *Star Trek* (NBC); *That Girl* (ABC).

Movies: *Alfie*; Lelouch's *A Man and a Woman*; *A Man for All Seasons* (Oscar); Antonioni's *Blow-Up*; *Georgy Girl*; *Who's Afraid of Virginia Woolf?*

Songs: "The Ballad of the Green Berets" (Barry Sadler); "I'm a Believer" (The Monkees); "Monday, Monday" (The Mamas and the Papas); "Sounds of Silence" (Simon and Garfunkel); "Winchester Cathedral" (New Vaudeville Band).

Books: *Human Sexual Response* (William Masters and Virginia Johnson); *In Cold Blood* (Truman Capote); *The Group* (Mary McCarthy); *On Aggression* (Konrad Lorenz); *Valley of the Dolls* (Jacqueline Susann).

Died: comic Lenny Bruce, 39; animator-impresario Walt Disney, 65; actor Buster Keaton, 70; satirist Evelyn Waugh, 62.

Debuts: National Organization for Women (NOW); Houston's Astrodome.

If **Barbara Bain** saw double **Martin Landau**s, it could only mean the couple (at the time married in real life) was off on another *Mission: Impossible*. They and cohorts Steven Hill, Greg Morris, and Peter Lupus used legerdemain, advanced technology, and a loud soundtrack to foil America's foe-of-the-week. Bain would win an Emmy each of her three years as a regular, half the series's total during its seven-year run.

His American dream curdling, Willie Loman (**Lee J. Cobb**, second from left) took it out on his family (**James Farentino**, **Mildred Dunnock**, and **George Segal**) in *Death of a Salesman*. The primetime staging of the piece that won playwright Arthur Miller a 1949 Pulitzer captured two Emmys, including one for best drama.

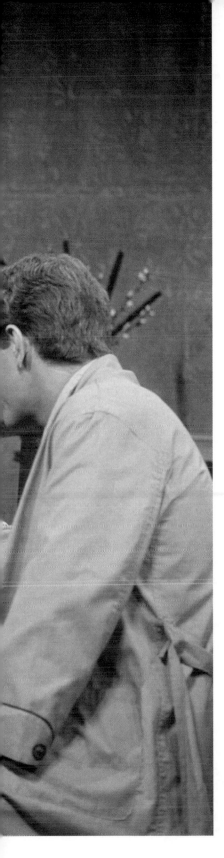

As the number of U.S. soldiers in Vietnam neared 400,000, **General William Westmoreland**, 52, met in Saigon with CBS Newsmen Charles Collingwood and Morley Safer; his optimistic take on the war formed the basis of a primetime special. In 1982, a CBS documentary would charge him with habitually underestimating enemy troop strength to maintain Congress's support. Westmoreland would file a $120-million libel suit but drop the action in mid-trial.

An Evening with Carol Channing, the saucer-eyed Broadway veteran's first primetime special, came on the heels of her Tony-winning turn in the smash musical *Hello, Dolly!* The 45-year-old star's guests: George Burns and an English actor not particularly noted for his woofing and hoofing, *The Man from U.N.C.L.E.*'s David McCallum.

Twenty-one years after it launched an unknown playwright named Tennessee Williams (who was born in Mississippi), *The Glass Menagerie* received a primetime production. **Shirley Booth** played the matriarch of a shabbily genteel Southern family, **Hal Holbrook** the restless son, and **Barbara Loden** the emotionally fragile daughter hoping for the best from suitor **Pat Hingle**.

How the Grinch Stole Christmas was the first network special drawn from the children's classics that Theodor Geisel penned as Dr. Seuss. Narrating this rhyme-happy tale of the holiday-saving Whos of Whoville: Boris Karloff.

In
Their
Own
Words

• • • • • • • •

RAYMOND BURR

Whose series ended after nine years, on the toll of carrying an hour-long dramatic show:

"I got up at three o'clock every morning to learn my lines for that day, and sometimes I didn't finish shooting until nine o'clock [at night]. That went on six days a week. I never went home— I lived on the lot. I had no life outside of *Perry Mason*."

Egypt and Syria invade Israel but lose "The Six-Day War." In the U.S., more than 125 cities are rocked by race riots. Protest marches against America's presence in Vietnam mount, and Muhammad Ali, 25, is stripped of his heavyweight title for refusing induction into the Army. In Super Bowl I, it's Green Bay 35, Kansas City 10.

Premiering series: *The Carol Burnett Show* (CBS); *The Flying Nun* (ABC); *Gentle Ben* (CBS); *Ironside* (NBC); *Love Is a Many Splendored Thing* (CBS); *Mannix* (CBS); *The Smothers Brothers Comedy Hour* (CBS); *The Forsyte Saga* (PBS).

Movies: Buñuel's *Belle de Jour*; *Bonnie and Clyde*; *The Dirty Dozen*; *The Graduate*; *In the Heat of the Night* (Oscar).

Songs: "Light My Fire" (The Doors); "Ode to Billie Joe" (Bobbie Gentry); "Respect" (Aretha Franklin); "Up Up and Away" (The Fifth Dimension); "White Rabbit" (The Jefferson Airplane).

Books: *The Naked Ape* (Desmond Morris); *One Hundred Years of Solitude* (Gabriel García Márquez); *The Outsiders* (S.E. Hinton); *Rosemary's Baby* (Ira Levin).

Died: Cuban revolutionary Che Guevera, 39; publisher Henry Luce, 68; singer Otis Redding, 26; actor Spencer Tracy, 67.

Debuts: heart transplantation (by Dr. Christiaan Barnard; first recipient Louis Washkansky lived 18 days); microwaves (by Amana); *Rolling Stone* magazine.

Since 1955, 10 P.M. Saturday on CBS had meant *Gunsmoke*. No more; when Marshall Dillon moseyed over to Monday night, his old time slot went to *Mannix*. Titular hero **Mike Connors** (right) was an L.A.-based private eye with a fondness for high-speed car chases and knuckle sandwiches; the action series spent three of its eight seasons in the Top 20.

The irreverence that won the **Smothers Brothers** a primetime variety show also cost them it. Comedic folksingers **Dick** (left) and **Tom** (right, with guest **Jimmy Durante**) had a nose for anti-Establishment material, especially songs and skits protesting the Vietnam War. *The Smothers Brothers Comedy Hour* was canceled after two seasons despite ratings high enough to unhorse NBC's *Bonanza* as TV's No. 1 show.

Hobbies rarely lead to Broadway and a primetime special. **Hal Holbrook**'s did. The veteran of stage and soap (CBS's *A Brighter Day*) turned his appreciation for a 19th-century American writer into a Tony-winning one-man show. Holbrook, 42, then reprised his recreation of the septuagenarian humorist Samuel L. Clemens in *Mark Twain Tonight!*

Two high-profile movements met when black militant **Stokely Carmichael** spoke at a peace rally. Riots sparked by perceived racial injustices were battering many cities, particularly Newark and Detroit. And marches against the U.S.'s Vietnam policy and its military draft were being staged from Oakland to Washington (where more than 50,000 protested at the Pentagon).

Carol Burnett had spent her late 20s as a second banana to Garry Moore. Now, at 34, the comedienne got to headline her own variety hour, and she slipped on no peels (unless the script called for it). Over the next 11 seasons *The Carol Burnett Show* would win four Emmys and the members of her repertory company—Harvey Korman, Vicki Lawrence, Lyle Waggoner, and, later, Tim Conway—another seven.

The frozen Wisconsin turf was as unyielding as concrete and the temperature minus-30 for the NFL championship game remembered as the "Ice Bowl." Host Green Bay's quarterback, Bart Starr, squirmed in for a last-gasp touchdown to beat the Dallas Cowboys. The Pack's reward? A trip to sunny Miami, where they dismantled the Oakland Raiders in Super Bowl II.

ANDY GRIFFITH

Whose show, after six seasons in Nielsen's Top 7, finally reached No. 1, on the appeal of his sitcom:

"Everybody has a hometown they either came from or they'd like to come from. Mayberry's the ideal hometown. Every problem could be solved in a half hour, usually by someone taking an interest in someone else."

At the lunar New Year, or Tet, the Viet Cong mount a widespread offensive that drives Lyndon Johnson's approval rating down to 26 percent. The incumbent declines to seek a new term; Richard M. Nixon defeats Hubert H. Humphrey to win the presidency. Striking workers and students paralyze France for three weeks. The Soviet Union sends tanks into Czechoslovakia to end liberal Alexander Dubcek's "Prague Spring."

Premiering Series : *The Archie Show* (CBS); *The Doris Day Show* (CBS); *Hawaii Five-0* (CBS); *Here's Lucy* (CBS); *Laugh-In* (NBC); *Mayberry, R.F.D.* (CBS); *Mister Rogers' Neighborhood* (PBS); *The Mod Squad* (ABC); *The Prisoner* (CBS); *60 Minutes* (CBS).

Movies: *Bullitt*; *Funny Girl*; *Planet of the Apes*; *The Odd Couple*; *Oliver!* (Oscar); *Rosemary's Baby*; *2001: A Space Odyssey*.

Songs: "Both Sides Now" (Judy Collins); "Do You Know the Way to San Jose" (Dionne Warwick); "I Heard It Through the Grapevine" (Marvin Gaye); "(Sittin' on) The Dock of the Bay" (Otis Redding).

Books: *Airport* (Arthur Hailey); *Soul on Ice* (Eldridge Cleaver); *The Whole Earth Catalog* (Stewart Brand).

Died: Senator Robert F. Kennedy, 42 (by assassination); the Reverend Martin Luther King Jr., 39 (by assassination); novelist John Steinbeck, 66.

Debuts: 911 emergency number; St. Louis's Gateway Arch; Jacuzzi whirlpool bath.

As sure as the majestic surf that was the show's aloha and the signature "Book him, Danno" that meant another arrest, star **Jack Lord** always remained unflappable (even when some desperado was mussing his coif). Paradise would find enough perps to keep the *Hawaii Five-0* crimebusters busy for 12 seasons—thereby tying *Dragnet* as TV's longest-running cop show.

Although U.S. troop strength in Vietnam was at an all-time high, the Viet Cong mounted a widescale offensive during Tet. CBS News anchor **Walter Cronkite**, 61, went in-country for a firsthand assessment. He concluded, in the primetime *Report from Vietnam by Walter Cronkite*, that to "this reporter" the war seemed "certain...to end in a stalemate." A month later, President Lyndon Johnson announced that his first full term would also be his last.

Coretta Scott King entered an Atlanta church not to hear her husband preach but to bury him. Four days earlier in Memphis, the Reverend Martin Luther King Jr., 39, had been gunned down by sniper James Earl Ray. King's nonviolent pursuit of racial equality had earned him the 1964 Nobel Peace prize; ironically, his assassination would set off riots in a number of American cities.

After a long night covering the pivotal California primaries, the CBS News staff in New York had powered down—only to regather after 3 A.M. when Democratic front-runner Robert F. Kennedy was shot minutes after claiming victory. Among those directing the network's special coverage: **Ernest Leiser** (fourth from left, wearing glasses), **Don Hewitt** (to the right of Leiser, wristwatch visible); CBS News president **Richard Salant** (behind man on phone, cigarette in hand), and **Bill Leonard** (to the right of Salant, wearing headphones), a future head of CBS News.

Part Kafka and part Lewis Carroll, *The Prisoner* was a 17-episode series that became an instant cult hit. **Patrick McGoohan** played a government spy abducted to a surrealistic British seaside resort from which there was no escape. Who were his fellow inmates? Who was the mute midget butler? Who were his captors and what did they want? All the paranoid plot lines converged in the two-part finale. Sort of.

Since autumn of 1965, CBS had scheduled documentaries and public-affairs programs at 10 P.M. on Tuesday. Now premiering in that time slot was the first network news-magazine: the biweekly *60 Minutes*, anchored by **Mike Wallace**, 50, and **Harry Reasoner**, 45. Three years later the show would move to early primetime on Sunday and in 1975 it would finally go weekly.

MIKE WALLACE

With Richard Nixon, on coaxing subjects to reveal themselves on 60 Minutes:

"You have to understand why they are doing the interview—you're giving them an opportunity to make their case. And you're not there to hit them. Rather, you have to establish a chemistry of confidentiality. Along the way, they become almost co-conspirators with you."

irst man on the moon: Neil Armstrong, 39. Golda Meir, 71, is Israel's first woman prime minister. Seven savage murders in Beverly Hills are pinned on Charles Manson's "family." The AFL wins its first Super Bowl: New York Jets 16, Baltimore Colts 7. Some 400,000 youths attend an outdoor musicfest near the New York town of Woodstock.

Premiering Series : *The Brady Bunch* (ABC); *The Glen Campbell Goodtime Hour* (CBS); *Hee-Haw* (CBS); *Marcus Welby, M.D.* (ABC); *Medical Center* (CBS); *Monty Python's Flying Circus* (PBS); *Room 222* (ABC); *Scooby-Doo* (CBS); *Sesame Street* (PBS).

Movies: *Butch Cassidy and the Sundance Kid*; *Easy Rider*; *Hello, Dolly!*; *Midnight Cowboy* (Oscar); *The Wild Bunch*; *Yellow Submarine*; Costa-Gavras's *Z*.

Songs: "Bad Moon Rising" (Creedence Clearwater Revival); "Everyday People" (Sly and the Family Stone); "I'll Be There" (The Jackson Five); "Lola" (The Kinks); "Sugar, Sugar" (The Archies).

Books: *The Godfather* (Mario Puzo); *On Death and Dying* (Elizabeth Kübler-Ross); *The French Lieutenant's Woman* (John Fowles); *Portnoy's Complaint* (Philip Roth).

Died: President Dwight Eisenhower, 78; entertainer Judy Garland, 47; North Vietnam leader Ho Chi Minh, 79; boxing's Rocky Marciano, 45 (in a plane crash).

Debuts: Concorde SST jet; *Doonesbury* (by cartoonist Garry Trudeau, 20); *Penthouse*.

Hee-Haw was *Laugh-In*'s down-home cousin, replete with manic pacing, one-line jokes, and a large cast of resident zanies. But hosts **Buck Owens** (with guitar) and **Roy Clark** (with banjo) also regularly presented top country-and-western musicians, a network rarity in a rock-driven era. Dropped after two seasons despite having placed in the Top 20 both years, *Hee-Haw* would continue in first-run syndication until 1993, making it the fifth most durable prime-time show ever.

Who needed the Beatles or the Beach Boys when the once-in-a-lifetime lineup included the Band, Janis, the Who, Jimi, Creedence Clearwater, Richie—and more? Max Yasgur's dairy farm, where some 400,000 young fans braved the rain for the weekend outdoor concert, actually lay in Bethel, New York. But the event was, is, and always will be known as Woodstock.

New York City pals **Paul Simon** and **Art Garfunkel**, both 28, had spent half their lives harmonizing. Three years after their breakout "Sounds of Silence" and two years after their seminal soundtrack for *The Graduate*, the duo made it to primetime by way of an hour-long special, *Songs of America*.

Smothers Brothers regular **Glen Campbell** proved a sufficiently winning host of a 1968 summer-replacement series to rate his own show. Many of *The Glen Campbell Goodtime Hour*'s musical guests were fellow rhinestone cowboys, but not all: **Stevie Wonder** was riding high on the pop charts with hits like "For Once in My Life" and "My Cherie Amour."

Six and a half hours earlier, the spacecraft *Eagle* had touched down on the lunar surface. Now, at 3:56 A.M. Greenwich Mean Time on July 21, astronaut **Neil Armstrong** neared the bottom of the module's ladder. A live audience of 600 million worldwide saw him plant his foot on the moon and heard his first words: "That's one small step for a man, one giant leap for mankind."

In the premiere episode of *Medical Center*, costar **Chad Everett** had to diagnose what ailed a guest star (Heisman trophy winner **O.J. Simpson**, 22, who in his day job was about to start his second season with the AFL Buffalo Bills). Everett and James Daly would anchor the hour-long hospital drama for seven seasons.

CHARLES KURALT

Winner of an Emmy for his On the Road *reports for CBS Evening News, on his assignment:*

"The little roads without numbers are the ones I have liked the best, the bumpy ones that lead over the hills toward vicinities unknown. I have attempted to keep 'relevance' and 'significance' out of the stories I send back. If I come upon a real news story out there, I call some real reporter to come cover it."

Președinte Nixon orders combat troops into neutral Cambodia; at a Kent State University protest rally, four students are shot dead by National Guardsmen. Margaret Smith Court, 28, wins tennis's Grand Slam. Americans can begin voting at 18. The Beatles disband.

Premiering series: *The Flip Wilson Show* (NBC); *The Mary Tyler Moore Show* (CBS); *NFL Monday Night Football* (ABC); *The Odd Couple* (ABC); *The Partridge Family* (ABC); *The Phil Donahue Show* (SYND); *Sabrina, the Teenage Witch* (CBS); *The Tim Conway Comedy Hour* (CBS).

Movies: *Airport*; *Five Easy Pieces*; *Love Story*; *M*A*S*H*; *Patton* (Oscar); Ophuls's *The Sorrow and the Pity*.

Songs: "Ain't No Mountain High Enough" (Diana Ross); "I Think I Love You" (The Partridge Family); "Knock Three Times" (Dawn); "Raindrops Keep Fallin' on My Head" (B.J. Thomas); "(They Long to Be) Close to You" (The Carpenters).

Books: *The Female Eunuch* (Germaine Greer); *Future Shock* (Alvin Toffler); *I Know Why the Caged Bird Sings* (Maya Angelou); *Love Story* (Erich Segal).

Died: French statesman Charles de Gaulle, 80; cartoonist Rube Goldberg, 87; rocker Jimi Hendrix, 27; singer Janis Joplin, 27; football's Vince Lombardi, 57.

Debuts: microprocessor (invented by Ted Hoff); fiber-optic cable; 747 jet; Gray Panthers (founded by Maggie Kuhn, 65).

After *The Dick Van Dyke Show*, **Mary Tyler Moore** tried Hollywood only to find her comedic brilliance wasted (she was cast as a nun in Elvis's *Change of Habit*). So at 32 the actress returned to primetime with *The Mary Tyler Moore Show*, a sitcom with an ensemble cast for the ages: **Ted Knight** as a blow-dried anchor, Ed Asner and Gavin MacLeod as newsroom colleagues, and Valerie Harper and Cloris Leachman as her Minneapolis neighbors.

Some 1,000 students at Kent State University in Kent, Ohio, had gathered for a noon rally to protest President Nixon's decision to bomb neutralist Cambodia. Armed Ohio National Guardsmen, who later testified they feared for their safety, unleashed tear gas and then a fusillade that left eight wounded and four dead (inset).

An al fresco concert along the banks of the Potomac River was one of the vignettes in the primetime special *A Day in the Life of the United States.* The particular day chosen by CBS News to send crews across the nation: July 20, 1969, when Neil Armstrong left man's first footprint on the moon.

Maybe some men really are from Mars...The age-old war between the sexes proved fertile sketch material for the **Anne Bancroft** special *Annie, the Women in the Life of a Man.* It was the 38-year-old star's first return to network television since the Golden Age of live drama; the show won a pair of Emmys.

Kids from around the world gathered at the United Nations in New York to say the darndest things to **Bill Cosby** on *A World of Love*, a special produced in conjunction with UNICEF. Joining the salute to the planet's young were cohost Shirley MacLaine and guest stars Audrey Hepburn, Harry Belafonte, and Julie Andrews.

MARY TYLER MOORE

on the Mary Richards who never made it on-air:

"Our first concept was to show her coming fresh from a broken marriage to start a new life in Minneapolis. The network said 'No, there's nothing funny about divorce.' Of course we've all seen that if handled in good taste, there's very little that can't be illuminated by comedy."

1971

The *New York Times* publishes the "Pentagon Papers," a classified history of the U.S.'s escalating involvement in Vietnam. Nationhood: Bangladesh. In Uganda, power is seized by Idi Amin Dada, 46. China joins the United Nations, replacing Taiwan.

Premiers series : *All in the Family* (CBS); *Cannon* (CBS); *Columbo* (NBC); *McMillan and Wife* (NBC); *The New Dick Van Dyke Show* (CBS); *Owen Marshall: Counselor at Law* (ABC); *The Sonny and Cher Comedy Hour* (CBS).

Movies: *A Clockwork Orange*; Bertolucci's *The Conformist*; *Dirty Harry*; *The French Connection* (Oscar); *Klute*; *McCabe & Mrs. Miller*; *Shaft*.

Songs: "Black Magic Woman" (Santana); "Joy to the World" (Three Dog Night); "Maggie May" (Rod Stewart); "Me and Bobby McGee" (Janis Joplin); "Proud Mary" (Ike and Tina Turner); "It's Too Late"/"I Feel the Earth Move" (Carole King).

Books: *Another Roadside Attraction* (Tom Robbins); *Bury My Heart at Wounded Knee* (Dee Brown); *In the Shadow of Man* (Jane Goodall).

Died: jazzman Louis Armstrong, 71; designer Coco Chanel, 86; golf's Bobby Jones, 69; rocker Jim Morrison, 27; retailer J.C. Penney, 95; composer Igor Stravinsky, 88.

Debuts: space station (the Soviet *Salyut I*); Greenpeace; a federal ban against advertising cigarettes on television.

They met doing backup vocals at a recording session and, after marriage, cut a string of hits that began with 1965's "I Got You Babe." But TV hosts? Few would have guessed that **Cher** Sarkisian, 25, was a natural comic and **Sonny Bono**, 36, her perfect foil. Alas, the beat would only go on for *The Sonny and Cher Comedy Hour* until 1974; the series was felled not by poor ratings but by the divorce of its stars.

The major tremor that shocked Los Angeles on February 10 did far worse than empty a supermarket's shelves: it killed some 60 people and injured 900. Casualties would have been even heavier had the earthquake, measuring 6.6 on the Richter scale, struck later in the day. But at 6 A.M., kids were still at home rather than in schools.

In-your-face comedy came to primetime with *All in the Family*, the breakthrough sitcom about a blue-collar patriarch not afraid to flaunt his bigotry (**Carroll O'Connor**, with **Mel Stewart**). Drawn from the British series *Til Death Us Do Part*, the show also starred **Jean Stapleton** (seated at table) as Archie Bunker's wife, Edith, and **Sally Struthers** and **Rob Reiner** (seated behind O'Connor's left shoulder) as their daughter, Gloria, and son-in-law, Meathead.

141

At the time he was cast as private eye *Cannon*, **William Conrad** (right, with guest **Fritz Weaver**) was best known for his off-camera voice. At 50, the actor had already created the role of Matt Dillon on radio's *Gunsmoke* in 1952 and narrated TV shows from *Rocky and Bullwinkle* to *The Fugitive*. Too portly to chase perps on foot, Conrad would nonetheless nab enough felons to enjoy a five-year run.

In *The Homecoming*, an original holiday tale, **Patricia Neal** played a rural matriarch and **Richard Thomas** the oldest of her seven children, an aspiring novelist named John-Boy. Scriptwriter Earl Hamner had previously dramatized his Depression-era childhood in the 1963 Henry Fonda movie *Spencer's Mountain*; he would continue to mine his past for the next nine years when CBS asked him to transform his Christmas-time special into *The Waltons*.

In
Their
Own
Words

• • • • • • • • •

ED SULLIVAN

*Whose variety show
finally closed, on
enduring 23 years
of jibes about his
wooden stage
demeanor:*

"Anybody who
says he is immune
to criticism is a
really big liar. You
don't get hardened
to it. Sure I've been
hurt by the jokes
about my act. I'm
accustomed to
them now but they
hurt. What I really
want, I guess, is
for people to tell
me I look like
Robert Goulet."

Richard M. Nixon defeats George S. McGovern to retain the presidency, despite a foiled burglary by GOP "plumbers" of Democratic offices in D.C.'s Watergate complex. At the Munich Olympics, Palestinian terrorists slay 11 Israeli athletes and coaches. Bobby Fischer defeats Boris Spassky for the world chess title. TV sets in use: 100 million.

Premiering series: *The Bob Newhart Show* (CBS); *Bridget Loves Bernie* (CBS); *Fat Albert and the Cosby Kids* (CBS); *Kung Fu* (ABC); *M*A*S*H* (CBS); *Maude* (CBS); *The Rookies* (ABC); *Sanford and Son* (NBC); *The Streets of San Francisco* (ABC); *The Waltons* (CBS).

Movies: *Cabaret*; *Deep Throat*; *Deliverance*; *The Godfather* (Oscar); Malle's *Murmur of the Heart*; *The Poseidon Adventure*.

Songs: "American Pie" (Don McLean); "The First Time Ever I Saw Your Face" (Roberta Flack); "I Am Woman" (Helen Reddy); "My Ding-a-Ling" (Chuck Berry); "Song Sung Blue" (Neil Diamond).

Books: *The Day of the Jackal* (Fredrick Forsyth); *The Exorcist* (William Blatty); *The Joy of Sex* (Alex Comfort).

Died: baseball's Roberto Clemente, 38 (on a mercy flight to earthquake-shattered Nicaragua); FBI czar J. Edgar Hoover, 77; poet Marianne Moore, 84; baseball's Jackie Robinson, 53; President Harry Truman, 88.

Debuts: San Francisco's BART and Washington's Metro subways; New York's World Trade Center; HBO; *Ms.* magazine.

Two years after Robert Altman scored a big-screen hit with the antiwar comedy *M*A*S*H*, the 4077th Mobile Army Surgical Hospital repitched its tents in a half-hour sitcom. Among the Korean War battlefield medicos under the command of **McLean Stevenson** (near right) were stars **Alan Alda** and **Wayne Rogers**. The transplant was a success: the series would run 11 years (eight more than the conflict that inspired it).

In its first season *The Waltons* won four Emmys, including one for best drama, while knocking TV's No. 2 series, *The Flip Wilson Show*, out of the Top 10. Its cast (from left, back row): Emmy winner **Michael Learned**, Emmy winner **Richard Thomas**, and **Ralph Waite**; (center row) **Jon Walmsley**, Emmy winner **Ellen Corby**, **Will Geer**, **Kami Cotler**, and **David W. Harper**; (front row) **Judy Norton Taylor**, **Eric Scott**, and **Elizabeth McDonough**.

Although the U.S. had not recognized Beijing since the People's Republic of China was founded in 1949, and although he had built his career on fighting Communism, **Richard Nixon** became the first president to visit the Mainland. When not conferring with Premier **Chou En-lai**, Nixon found time to play tourist. Gazing up at China's best-known wonder, he said in astonishment, "This is a great wall!"

Introduced on *All in the Family* as a liberal sparring partner for Archie Bunker, Broadway veteran **Bea Arthur**, 46, roared off with her own spin-off show. **Adrienne Barbeau** costarred as *Maude*'s daughter and Bill Macy as Hubby No. 4. During its six-year run, the sitcom would court controversy by finding humor in themes like abortion, alcoholism, and menopause.

Your average psychologist frowns on patients who clown around. **Bob Newhart** was not your average psychologist. Venturing into his first sitcom after a storied career in stand-up, the comedian, 42, and a supporting cast led by Suzanne Pleshette would continue *The Bob Newhart Show*'s weekly laughter therapy for six years.

Fat Albert and the Cosby Kids sprang from Bill Cosby's comic monologues about the Philadelphia neighborhood in which he grew up in the 1940s. The animated series, featuring childhood pals like Fat Albert, Mush Mouth, and Weird Harold, would be a Saturday-morning fixture for a dozen years, then continue in syndication for another five.

In
Their
Own
Words

• • • • • • • • •

Carol Burnett

Whose show won the first of its three Emmys for best variety series, on a rather daredevil wish that never came to pass:

"I would do my show live in a minute if we had a proper theater. People make mistakes, but then find things to bail themselves out and keep the audience with them."

1973

Washington and Hanoi agree to a cease-fire in Vietnam. Chile's Marxist president, Salvador Allende, dies in a CIA-backed coup. Egypt and Syria lead an attack on Israel on Yom Kippur but are repelled; OPEC promptly doubles the price of crude oil. President Nixon fires top aides as Watergate probers learn of a secret White House taping system. Vice President Spiro Agnew resigns for evading income taxes; he is replaced by Gerry Ford. In *Roe* v. *Wade*, the U.S. Supreme Court deems abortions legal. The Miami Dolphins win Super Bowl VII to finish 17-0. UCLA wins the NCAA basketball title to finish 32-0.

Premiering series: *Barnaby Jones* (CBS); *Kojak* (CBS); *Police Story* (NBC); *The Six Million Dollar Man* (ABC); *The Young and the Restless* (CBS).

Movies: *American Graffiti*; *The Exorcist*; *Paper Moon*; *Serpico*; *The Sting* (Oscar); *The Way We Were*.

Songs: "Crocodile Rock" (Elton John); "Rocky Mountain High" (John Denver); "Tie a Yellow Ribbon Round the Ole Oak Tree" (Dawn); "Time in a Bottle" (Jim Croce); "You're So Vain" (Carly Simon).

Books: *The Best and the Brightest* (David Halberstam); *Fear of Flying* (Erica Jong).

Died: director John Ford, 78; President Lyndon Johnson, 64; *Pogo* creator Walt Kelly, 60; artist Pablo Picasso, 92.

Debuts: UPC bar code; baseball's designated hitter (in the American League only).

In *Lily Tomlin*, the 32-year-old comedienne delved into her repertoire for such personae as little Edith Ann and Ernestine ("one ringy-dingy, two ringy-dingies"), Telephone Operator from Hell. Her show, guest-starring Richard Pryor, won two Emmys, including for best comedy-variety special.

The failed 1972 break-in at Democratic National Headquarters may indeed have been, in the words of a Richard Nixon aide, "a third-rate burglary." But a Senate hearing exposed a White House cover-up. Star witness of the televised sessions: **John Dean** (whose wife **Mo** was often in attendance). President Nixon's ex-counsel told the Ervin subcommittee he had warned his boss that Watergate was becoming "a cancer on the presidency."

A private investigator virtually eligible for Social Security who preferred a glass of milk to a shot of whiskey? Why not, if he was portrayed by **Buddy Ebsen** (with guest **Carl Betz**)? As L.A.-based *Barnaby Jones,* the erstwhile Jed Clampett cracked cases with the help of an elaborate at-home forensics lab. By the time the series left the air, two years short of *The Beverly Hillbillies*'s run, its star would be 72.

Lauren Bacall had snapped out of a personal and professional funk by hitting the boards in *Applause*, a 1970 Broadway musical adapted from *All About Eve*. The actress—at 46 celebrating a quarter-century in show business—recreated her Tony award–winning role in a primetime special.

The Young and the Restless evolved into the top-rated daytime soap by adding action to the oft-static genre, as when a thug took forcible possession of a car belonging to **Tom Hallick** (later an original co-anchor of the syndicated *Entertainment Tonight*). Other actors who can claim the show on their résumés: Sharon Farrell, Deidre Hall, David Hasselhoff, and Tom Selleck.

Having made his mark as a hardened con in *Birdman of Alcatraz* and a psycho soldier in *The Dirty Dozen*, Aristotle (**Telly**) Savalas, 48, seemed an unlikely leading man. But his turn as a sardonic, lollipop-devouring New York detective in a March telefilm, *The Marcus-Nelson Murders*, led to a series that premiered in October. Who loves ya, baby? The Emmy voters, who named Savalas best actor for *Kojak*.

● ● ● ● ● ● ●

RICHARD THOMAS

Who picked up a best leading actor Emmy for The Waltons, on preparing himself to play John-Boy:

"I'm from West 96th Street in New York City but my ties to the rural life are real. My father was born in Muddy Branch, Kentucky, where Grandpa was elected the first mayor."

Impeached by the House for abetting the Watergate cover-up, Richard Nixon resigns his presidency rather than face a Senate trial. His successor: Gerald R. Ford. Kidnapped heiress Patty Hearst, 19, resurfaces as a bank robber. Muhammad Ali, 32, regains his boxing crown. Henry Aaron hits homer No. 715.

Premiering series: *Chico and the Man* (NBC); *Good Times* (CBS); *Happy Days* (ABC); *Little House on the Prairie* (NBC); *The Night Stalker* (ABC); *Police Woman* (NBC); *Rhoda* (CBS); *The Rockford Files* (NBC).

Movies: *Alice Doesn't Live Here Anymore*; *Blazing Saddles*; *Chinatown*; *The Conversation*; *Earthquake*; *The Godfather Part II* (Oscar); *Lenny*; *The Towering Inferno*.

Songs: "Band on the Run" (Paul McCartney and Wings); "Kung Fu Fighting" (Carl Douglas); "Midnight at the Oasis" (Maria Muldaur); "Seasons in the Sun" (Terry Jacks); "Sweet Home Alabama" (Lynyrd Skynyrd); "The Way We Were" (Barbra Streisand).

Books: *Looking for Mr. Goodbar* (Judith Rossner); *All the President's Men* (Bob Woodward and Carl Bernstein); *The Gulag Archipelago* (Vol. 1) (Aleksandr Solzhenitsyn); *Jaws* (Peter Benchley).

Died: comedian Jack Benny, 80; jazz's Duke Ellington, 75; singer Cass Elliot, 31; aviator Charles Lindbergh, 73; German industrialist Oskar Schindler, 66; TV host Ed Sullivan, 73.

Debuts: Heimlich hug; *People* magazine.

Six years earlier, **Richard Nixon** had become the first American in 128 years to capture the White House after losing a previous general election. Two years earlier, he had won a second term by a record landslide. Now, after more than a year of hearings into his role in deflecting a full investigation of Watergate, the 37th president became the first to resign. A month later Nixon, 61, was granted a full and unconditional pardon by his successor, Gerald Ford.

6 Rms Riv Vu—New York real-estate short-hand for a must-have apartment—was also the title of a Broadway play by Bob Randall. In the version staged for CBS, **Carol Burnett** and **Alan Alda** portrayed two strangers, each enduring a so-so marriage, who arrive to inspect the place and are drawn to each other.

After two seasons portraying Maude's maid, **Esther Rolle** (second from left) won her own spin-off series. In *Good Times,* **John Amos** (left) played her husband and **Jimmie Walker** (center) and **Ralph Carter** her sons; **Ja'net DuBois** was the best-friend neighbor. The sit-com's inaugural year was, in Walker's familiar catchphrase, "Dy-No-Mite"; it finished No. 8 in the Nielsens.

So in Minneapolis, who needs a subway token to get married? But leaving *The Mary Tyler Moore Show* after four years to dress windows in New York paid two quick dividends for **Valerie Harper.** Episode 8 of *Rhoda,* in which she and Joe (David Groh) were wed, drew a then-record 50 million viewers. And the actress, 34, added to her three supporting Emmys with one for Lead Actress in a Comedy Series.

Fresh from her Oscar-nominated role in
Sounder, **Cicely Tyson,** 40, gave a tour-de-
force performance in *The Autobiography of
Miss Jane Pittman.* The telemovie was based
on a novel by Ernest J. Gaines and filmed on
location in New Orleans. It traced one
woman's life from the Civil War to the 1960s
to show her triumph over Jim Crow prejudice. Tyson, whose character was required to
age from 19 to 111, took home two of the
special's nine Emmys.

At 40, she had appeared in 28 movies and
written one best-seller (1970's *Don't Fall Off
the Mountain*). But for her first primetime
special, she went back to her showbiz roots:
the chorus lines that launched her career. The
resulting musical was the Emmy-winning
Shirley MacLaine: If They Could See Me Now.

ALAN ALDA

Who collected the first two of his five M*A*S*H Emmys, on the theme he felt was the show's most powerful:

"There is no human drive more powerful than friendship. Oh, well yes, the sex drive is more powerful, I suppose, but it's relatively uncomplicated when you engage in it. Friendship can be a lot more difficult."

Seventeen hours after the last U.S. Marines evacuate Saigon, North Vietnamese troops take over and rename it Ho Chi Minh City. Teamsters boss Jimmy Hoffa, 61, vanishes. In China's Shenshi province archeologists find a royal tomb, sealed in 206 B.C., guarded by 6,000 life-sized terra cotta warriors.

Premiering series: *Barney Miller* (ABC); *The Bionic Woman* (ABC); *The Jeffersons* (CBS); *One Day at a Time* (CBS); *Phyllis* (CBS); *Saturday Night Live* (NBC); *Starsky and Hutch* (ABC); *Welcome Back, Kotter* (ABC).

Movies: *Jaws*; *The Man Who Would Be King*; *Nashville*; *One Flew Over the Cuckoo's Nest* (Oscar); *The Rocky Horror Picture Show*; *Shampoo*.

Songs: "Love Will Keep Us Together" (Captain and Tennille); "Lovin' You" (Minnie Ripperton); "Mandy" (Barry Manilow); "Rhinestone Cowboy" (Glen Campbell); "That's the Way (I Like It)" (KC and the Sunshine Band).

Books: *Looking for Mr. Goodbar* (Judith Rossner); *Ragtime* (E.L. Doctorow); *Shogun* (James Clavell).

Died: Spanish dictator Francisco Franco, 82; dramatist Rod Serling, 50; playwright Thornton Wilder, 78.

Debuts: VCR (Sony's Betamax); build-it-yourself personal computer (MITS Altair kit, sold by Ed Roberts); MS-DOS (from Microsoft cofounders Bill Gates, 20, and Paul Allen, 22); Post-it notes; Pet Rocks.

It wasn't Archie Bunker's tirades that drove away his *All in the Family* neighbors, irascible George Jefferson (**Sherman Hemsley**) and long-suffering wife, Louise (**Isabel Sanford**). It was the couple's thriving dry-cleaning business, their desire to move from Queens to Manhattan—and their shot at a spin-off series. *The Jeffersons* would finish in the Top 20 in half its 10 years, during which Sanford won an Emmy, in 1981.

Fending off amorous apartment super-intendent **Pat Harrington** was the least of divorcée **Bonnie Franklin's** worries on *One Day at a Time*. She also had to single-parent two teenage daughters (Mackenzie Phillips and Valerie Bertinelli). During the sitcom's nine-season run, it would place in Nielsen's Top 12 five times.

Start with a feisty young heroine created by one of America's most honored author-illustrators of children's books. Add a score by Grammy-winning composer-singer Carole (*Tapestry*) King. The resulting primetime special? *Maurice Sendak's Really Rosie.*

The original *Babe* was no pig; from the 1930s until her death in 1956, she was America's most renowned woman athlete, excelling in track and field, tennis, golf, and even baseball. **Susan Clark**, 32, won an Emmy for her portrayal of Mildred (Babe) Didrikson Zaharias. Playing her husband was ex-NFL lineman Alex Karras, whom Clark would later marry and costar with in the sitcom *Webster*.

Stage veteran **Maureen Stapleton,** 51, and character actor **Charles Durning,** 50, were a wistful romantic duo in *Queen of the Stardust Ballroom.* She played a recently widowed Bronx housewife seeking companionship at a dance hall; he played a postman who, alas, was married. In the acclaimed telemovie, the couple expressed their growing affection for each other in an innovative way: via musical soliloquies.

The plot device to spin off a second series from *The Mary Tyler Moore Show* was grief. In the premiere of *Phyllis,* the death of her husband (the never-seen Lars) prompted **Cloris Leachman** to move with daughter **Lisa Gerritsen** to San Francisco. The sitcom would never recover from an off-screen tragedy, the murder of supporting actress Barbara Colby after her appearance in just the first episode.

• • • • • • • • •

VALERIE HARPER

On the medium of television:

"Let's face it, Rhoda is what made the rest of my career possible. I'm not one of those actors who talks constantly about escaping from television. I'd rather do the finest in television than some mediocre Broadway play or grade-C movie."

In the year America turns 200, Jimmy (James E.) Carter defeats Gerald R. Ford for the presidency. Israeli commandos free 104 hostages held in Uganda by pro-Palestinian skyjackers. Romanian gymnast Nadia Comaneci, 14, posts the Olympics's first "10" while winning three golds in Montreal.

Premiering series: *Alice* (CBS); *Charlie's Angels* (ABC); *Delvecchio* (CBS); *Family* (ABC); *Laverne and Shirley* (ABC); *The MacNeil-Lehrer Report* (PBS); *Mary Hartman, Mary Hartman* (SYND); *The Muppet Show* (SYND); *Quincy, M.E.* (NBC); *Wonder Woman* (ABC).

Movies: *All the President's Men*; Annaud's *Black and White in Color*; *Carrie*; *King Kong* (with Jessica Lange); *Network*; *Rocky* (Oscar); *Taxi Driver*.

Songs: "Bohemian Rhapsody" (Queen); "Disco Duck (Part 1)" (Rick Dees and His Cast of Idiots); "Love to Love You Baby" (Donna Summer); "This Masquerade" (George Benson); "You Should Be Dancing" (The Bee Gees).

Books: *The Hite Report* (Shere Hite); *Roots* (Alex Haley); *The Uses of Enchantment* (Bruno Bettelheim).

Died: sculptor Alexander Calder, 78; mystery queen Agatha Christie, 85; tycoon Howard Hughes, 70; novelist André Malraux, 75; Chinese leader Mao Tse-tung, 82.

Debuts: female cadets at the three U.S. service academies; Apple I computer (from Steve Wozniak, 23, and Steve Jobs, 21).

Steve Railsback portrayed apocalyptic cultist Charles Manson, accused with three disciples (**Christina Hart**, near right, **Marilyn Burns**, and **Cathey Paine**) of the 1969 rampage that left seven slaughtered in Beverly Hills, including pregnant actress Sharon Tate. The four-hour miniseries *Helter Skelter* was based on the nonfiction bestseller by Vincent Bugliosi, the Los Angeles prosecutor who put the four "Family" members behind bars for life.

By the time he got to Phoenix, guest **George Burns** was delighted to find *Alice*'s restaurant right there. Actually he was in Mel's Diner, where series star **Linda Lavin** (left) and **Polly Holliday** slung hash for **Vic Tayback.** Based on 1975's *Alice Doesn't Live Here Anymore*, featuring Oscar-winner Ellen Burstyn and Tayback as Mel, the sitcom would place in the Top 12 five times during its nine-year run.

Why did *Delvecchio* join the LAPD? Because he flunked the state bar exam. Star **Judd Hirsch,** 41, had won acclaim in dramas like *The Law*, a 1974 telemovie, and subsequent miniseries, but his first weekly show lasted only one season. So who could blame him for moving to New York to drive taxis?

U.S.C.G.C. EAGLE

To properly cover a birthday party 200 years in the making, CBS News preempted regular programming on the Fourth of July for the 16-hour special *In Celebration of US*. Highlights: **Charles Kuralt** at New York's Operation Sail, featuring a parade of 15 "tall ships" flanked by a 200-strong armada; a restaging of the Battle of Gettysburg; and Bicentennial fireworks coast-to-coast.

171

Enjoying a stogie at the local pool hall was a real change of pace for the character played by **Ralph Waite** in *The Secret Life of John Chapman*. The telemovie was based on the memoirs of a college president who took a sabbatical to sample life beyond the ivied halls. His jobs were all blue-collar—but then there were no faculty teas to attend.

The night Jimmy Carter won a term in the White House marked the eighth and final Election Night to feature **Eric Sevareid**'s political analysis. Recruited to CBS by Edward R. Murrow in 1939 to report (via radio) from France, he switched to television nine years later. Sevareid contributed commentaries to the *CBS Evening News* from the 1960s until 1977, and in retirement would serve as a consultant to CBS News until his death in 1992, at age 79.

• • • • • • •

JEAN STAPLETON

and

CARROLL O'CONNOR

Whose All in the Family *had just topped the Nielsens for a fifth straight year, on working with each other:*

Stapleton: "He's marvelously cultured, with an erudite mind."

O'Connor: "She's a gem."

Stapleton: "We've played together so long, we're like the Lunts."

Egyptian President Anwar Sadat visits Jerusalem to discuss Mideast peace with Israeli Prime Minister Menachem Begin. Two 747 jumbo jets packed with vacationers collide on a foggy runway in the Canary Islands, killing 583. America is transfixed for eight straight evenings by the ABC miniseries *Roots*.

Premiering series: *Carter Country* (ABC); *CHiPs* (NBC); *Eight Is Enough* (ABC); *Lou Grant* (CBS); *The Love Boat* (ABC); *Soap* (ABC); *Three's Company* (ABC).

Movies: *Annie Hall* (Oscar); *Close Encounters of the Third Kind*; *Julia*; Mizrahi's *Madame Rosa*; *Saturday Night Fever*; *Smokey and the Bandit*; *Star Wars*.

Songs: "Don't It Make My Brown Eyes Blue" (Crystal Gayle); "Don't Stop" (Fleetwood Mac); "Hotel California" (The Eagles); "Margaritaville" (Jimmy Buffett); "You Light Up My Life" (Debby Boone); "You Make Me Feel Like Dancing" (Leo Sayer).

Books: *All Things Wise and Wonderful* (James Herriot); *The Thorn Birds* (Colleen McCullough).

Died: actor Charlie Chaplin, 88; actress Joan Crawford, 73; crooner Bing Crosby, 73; funnyman Groucho Marx, 86; novelist Vladimir Nabokov, 78; rock's Elvis Presley, 42; comic Freddie Prinze, 22 (by suicide).

Debuts: the 799-mile trans-Alaskan oil pipeline; space shuttle (*Enterprise* passes its first test flight); Snugli baby carrier.

The Mary Tyler Moore Show exited as it had entered: laughing. WJM-TV regulars **Betty White**, **Gavin MacLeod**, **Ed Asner**, **Georgia Engel**, **Ted Knight**, and **Mary Tyler Moore** may have been lovable, but their shows pulled abysmal ratings. Which was why new management decided to issue wholesale pink slips; only Knight's self-absorbed announcer survived to turn off the lights on the sitcom's 168th and last episode.

After 18 months of hopscotching ABC's schedule, **Lynda Carter** flew her gravity-defying superheroine over to a weekly CBS series. Only costar Lyle Waggoner went with her. The show got a fresh title (*The New Adventures of Wonder Woman*) and fresh villains (modern-day terrorists instead of Nazis). Gone too was her kid sis Drusilla, Debra Winger having opted to try her luck in movies.

Freedom was **Alan Arkin**'s goal in *The Defection of Simas Kudirka*, based on a Cold War incident. In 1970, when a Soviet trawler entered U.S. waters, a seaman leapt across to a Coast Guard cutter and requested asylum. Washington tripped over its own red tape and allowed Kudirka to be hauled back to his own ship; but he eventually won the right to stay. The Emmy-winning telemovie costarred **Shirley Knight**.

Sacked from video journalism in Minneapolis, *Lou Grant* recovered nicely by landing on a Los Angeles daily newspaper. In the *Mary Tyler Moore Show* spin-off, **Ed Asner** retained his amusingly gruff persona, but the hour-long show was less interested in jokes than in probing topical real-life issues like gun control and child abuse. During its five seasons it would win eight Emmys, including for best dramatic series in 1979.

The Amazing Howard Hughes proved a career breakthrough for **Tommy Lee Jones**. Though only 31, he portrayed the legendary Texas billionaire who descended from robust wheeler-dealer to phobia-ridden recluse at his death at 71. The four-hour telemovie sprang the Harvard-educated actor from B-movies (1976's *Jackson County Jail*) into features like 1980's *Coal Miner's Daughter*, for which Jones won his first Oscar nomination.

It was on August 16 that **Elvis** left the building. Found comatose in his Graceland home, The King's long battle with drugs and obesity ended hours later in a Memphis hospital. Though only 42, Presley had redefined the popular culture by taking rock mainstream. The primetime special *Elvis in Concert*, filmed weeks earlier, captured his weakening health—and his immortal music.

BEA ARTHUR

Who collected an Emmy for Maude, *on becoming a late-blooming primetime star:*

"My training has been total I've done everything except rodeos and stag movies. My first Equity job was as Tallulah Bankhead's under-study. She was referred to as 'madam.' Now, I'm 'madam.'"

F ollowing the deaths of Paul VI and John Paul I (after only 34 days as pope), the Catholic Church elects its first non-Italian pontiff since A.D. 1523: John Paul II (Poland's Karol Wojtyla, 68). In Jonestown, Guyana, 913 disciples of faith-healer Jim Jones, 47, die by drinking a poisoned beverage (or are killed for refusing to). Janet Guthrie, 29, qualifies to race in the Indianapolis 500.

Premiering series: *Dallas* (CBS); *Diff'rent Strokes* (NBC); *Fantasy Island* (ABC); *The Incredible Hulk* (CBS); *Kaz* (CBS); *Mork and Mindy* (ABC); *The Paper Chase* (CBS); *Taxi* (ABC); *20/20* (ABC); *The White Shadow* (CBS); *WKRP in Cincinnati* (CBS).

Movies: *Animal House*; *The Buddy Holly Story*; *The Deer Hunter* (Oscar); *Grease*; *Halloween*; *Superman*; *An Unmarried Woman*.

Songs: "Just the Way You Are" (Billy Joel); "Last Dance" (Donna Summer); "Take a Chance on Me" (Abba); "Three Times a Lady" (The Commodores); "You're the One That I Want" (John Travolta and Olivia Newton-John).

Books: *A Distant Mirror* (Barbara Tuchman); *Mommie Dearest* (Christina Crawford); *Scruples* (Judith Krantz).

Died: surrealist Giorgio de Chirico, 90; mathematician Kurt Gödel, 71; Israeli stateswoman Golda Meir, 80; illustrator Norman Rockwell, 84.

Debuts: in vitro, or test-tube-conceived, human (England's Louise Brown).

Empathy was not **Larry Hagman**'s forte on *Dallas*, except perhaps when dad **Jim Davis** suffered a heart attack; his J.R. Ewing was usually cruder than the oil he pumped. The hour-long primetime soap, set in petrodollar-flush Texas, pulled middling ratings its first year. Then the South Fork back-stabbers would move to Friday night—and dominate the Nielsens for much of a run that lasted until 1991.

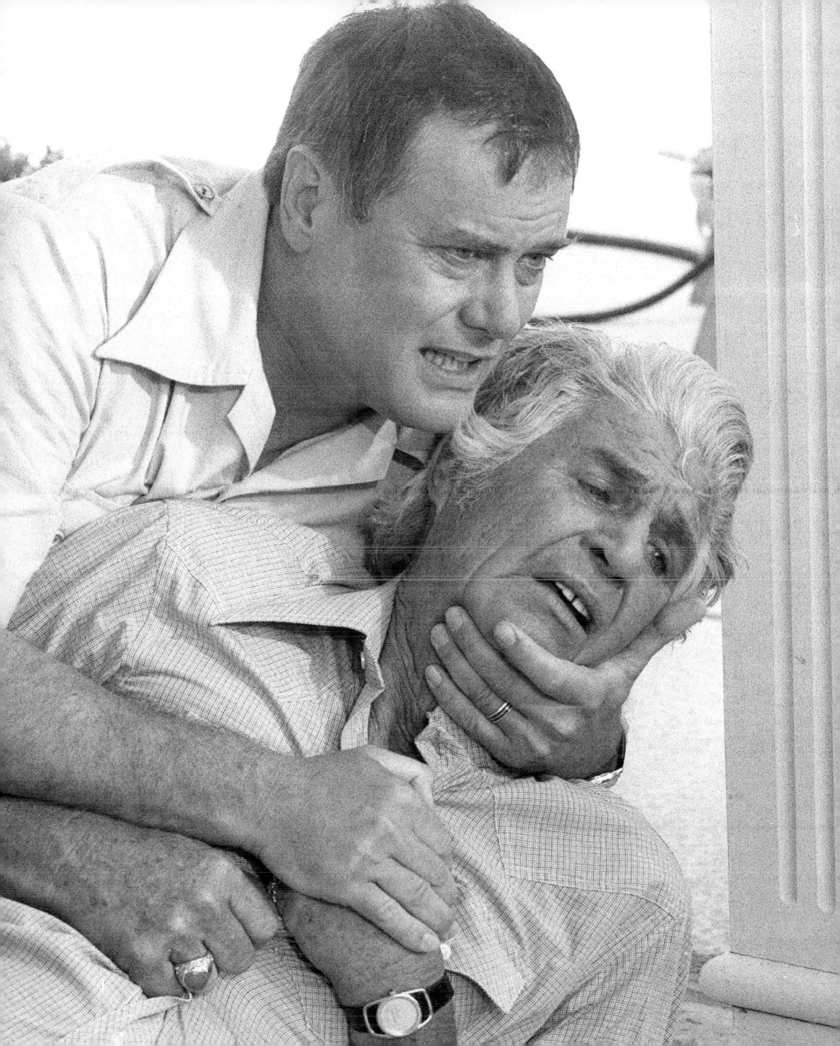

Sight gags on radio? Yes, if the studio was
WKRP in Cincinnati, where DJs like **Howard
Hesseman** enjoyed titillating secretary **Loni
Anderson**. The sitcom, about a station in
format transition from middle-of-the-road
to rock, would remain on-air for four seasons.

The largest recorded mass suicide of the 20th century took place in Jonestown, founded by cult leader Jim Jones in the jungles of Guyana. After camp guards murdered an inquiring U.S. congressman (plus an aide and two journalists), Jones ordered his mostly American disciples to drink cyanide-laced Fla-Vor-Aid. He then put a gun to his own head. Total dead: 916.

In the year that Jim Fixx's best-seller, *The Complete Book of Running*, ignited a jogging craze, **Joanne Woodward** played a teacher who worked off domestic tensions by lacing up. In the telemovie *See How She Runs* the actress, 47, struggled to complete the Boston Marathon; with Emmy voters, though, she finished first.

The Incredible Hulk was one green giant who rarely chortled "Ho-ho-ho." A former Mr. America, **Lou Ferrigno,** played the not-so-jolly muscleboy who emerged whenever mild-mannered series star Bill Bixby became enraged. Why the big morph? There was this accident in a research lab, see, and...

Previous U.S. administrations had tried to achieve a Mideast detente through shuttle diplomacy. President **Jimmy Carter** simplified the logistics by inviting Egypt's **Anwar Sadat** (left) and Israel's **Menachem Begin** to Camp David, where he acted as their personal intermediary. After 13 days of negotiations, the two bitter rivals shook hands and agreed to initiate peace talks.

. . . .

BOB
NEWHART

*On his
Milquetoast image:*

"I'd love to play
a tough-talking
gunslinger in a
Western. But the
minute I came
through the
swinging doors,
the audience
would be
hysterical."

Shah Reza Pahlevi cedes Iran to Ayatollah Khomeini, whose Shi'ite followers seize the U.S. Embassy in Tehran, along with 53 hostages. Anastasio Somoza Debayle cedes Nicaragua to Daniel Ortega's Sandinista rebels. Margaret Thatcher, 54, is Britain's first woman prime minister. An accident at the Three Mile Island nuclear power plant near Middletown, Pennsylvania, causes a near-meltdown. The U.S.S.R. dispatchs 40,000 troops to subdue Afghanistan.

Premiering series: *Benson* (ABC); *The Dukes of Hazzard* (CBS); *The Facts of Life* (NBC); *Hart to Hart* (ABC); *Knots Landing* (CBS); *Trapper John, M.D.* (CBS).

Movies: *Apocalypse Now*; *The China Syndrome*; *Kramer vs. Kramer* (Oscar); *Norma Rae*; *Star Trek: The Motion Picture*; *10*.

Songs: "Escape (The Piña Colada Song)" (Rupert Holmes); "The Gambler" (Kenny Rogers); "Heart of Glass" (Blondie); "My Sharona" (The Knack); "Y.M.C.A." (The Village People).

Books: *Complete Scarsdale Medical Diet* (Herman Tarnower); *The Right Stuff* (Tom Wolfe); *The Road Less Traveled* (M. Scott Peck); *Sophie's Choice* (William Styron).

Died: conductor Arthur Fiedler, 84; clown Emmett Kelly, 81; director Jean Renoir, 85; singer Minnie Riperton, 31; actress Jean Seberg, 40; actor John Wayne, 72.

Debuts: Sony Walkman; ESPN; Moral Majority (founded by Jerry Falwell, 41).

Slapstick car chases down the back roads of mythical Hazzard County jumped *The Dukes of Hazzard* into the Top 10 its first three seasons. Those stunts were costly; the producers totaled an average of three vehicles per show. The road-running Duke clan included (inset, from left) **Catherine Bach**, **Tom Wopat**, **John Schneider**; vanilla-suited **Sorrell Booke**, and **James Best** played the hapless foils.

Ten months after forcing their Shah to flee Iran, Islamic militants loyal to the Ayatollah Khomeini seized the U.S. Embassy in Tehran. The act was payback for the White House decision to allow the cancer-stricken Shah to seek treatment in New York. Though the militants did free a few female and black embassy staffers, they would keep 52 Americans hostage for 444 days, dooming a second term for Jimmy Carter.

Trapper John had been scripted out of *M*A*S*H* in 1975 when Wayne Rogers quit the show. He returned to primetime in the older, portlier, and balder form of **Pernell Roberts** (right); but then, this hour-long drama was set in San Francisco a full quarter-century after Korea. *Trapper John, M.D.* regulars aiding fallen guest star **James Coco**: **Gregory Harrison** (left), nurse **Christopher Norris**, and **Simon Scott**.

Katharine Hepburn, 71, traveled to North Wales to reunite with director George Cukor on *The Corn Is Green*, in which she played a strong-willed schoolmarm set on bringing literacy to a poor mining town. The tele-movie was adapted from an Emlyn Williams play that also served as the basis for a 1945 theatrical starring Bette Davis.

Michele Lee could stand up for herself at the beach; it was the bedrooms of *Knots Landing* that spelled trouble. The *Dallas* spin-off was created to give the lamest Ewing brother, Gary (Ted Shackelford), new ways to fail. So entertaining was this soap's take on lust, greed, and venality among coastal Californians that it would run 14 seasons—one more than its parent show.

Diahann Carroll (with young **Constance Good**) headed an exceptional cast of black actresses in *I Know Why the Caged Bird Sings*; the telemovie costarred Ruby Dee, Esther Rolle, and Madge Sinclair. It was adapted from Maya Angelou's 1970 memoirs, in which the author came to terms with a childhood in Depression-era Dixie complicated by the divorce of her parents.

Ronald W. Reagan defeats Jimmy Carter for the presidency. America's hockey team wins a surprise gold medal at Lake Placid but the U.S. and 61 other nations boycott the Moscow Summer Olympics to protest the Soviet invasion of Afghanistan. Shipworkers in Poland go on strike, led by Lech Walesa, 37. Mount St. Helens in Washington, dormant in this century, erupts. Japan's Sadaharu Oh, 40, lays down his bat after 868 home runs in 22 years. A record 86.6 million turn on *Dallas* to learn who shot J.R.

Premiering series: *ABC News Nightline* (ABC); *Bosom Buddies* (ABC); *Flo* (CBS); *Magnum, P.I.* (CBS).

Movies: *Airplane!*, *The Elephant Man*; Menshov's *Moscow Does Not Believe in Tears*; *Nine to Five*; *Ordinary People* (Oscar); *Raging Bull*; *Urban Cowboy*.

Songs: "Another One Bites the Dust" (Queen); "Fame" (Irene Cara); "On the Road Again" (Willie Nelson); "The Rose" (Bette Midler); "Sailing" (Christopher Cross); "Whip It" (Devo).

Books: *Cosmos* (Carl Sagan); *Innocent Blood* (P.D. James); *The Right Stuff* (Tom Wolfe).

Died: director Alfred Hitchcock, 80; singer John Lennon, 40 (shot by a stalker); actor Steve McQueen, 50; pollster A.C. Nielsen, 83; track's Jesse Owens, 66; actress Mae West, 87.

Debuts: CNN; Rollerblades.

The four-hour docudrama *Guyana Tragedy: The Story of Jim Jones* aired just 16 months after the gruesome mass suicide at Jonestown. For his portrayal of the charismatic preacher, who had moved his People's Temple from the Bay Area to South America to avoid arrest, 31-year-old **Powers Boothe** won an Emmy.

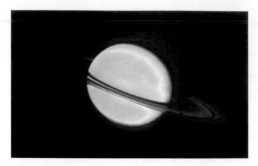

Thirty-eight months and 807 million miles after *Voyager II*'s launch, the space probe beamed back extraordinarily detailed photographs of Saturn. The ring circling the 6th rock from the Sun turns out to be less than 10 miles thick, yet extends 35,000 miles into space. In addition, the planet is circled by at least 22 satellites, more than double the number observable from Earth.

At 35, **Tom Selleck** had worked in B-movies (*Daughters of Satan, Gypsy Warriors*) and modeled in commercials. That all changed with *Magnum, P.I.* The series, in which Selleck played a Naval Intelligence Vietvet turned Hawaii-based private eye, would rank as high as No. 3 during its eight-year run. The only drawback: he had to turn down the lead in *Raiders of the Lost Ark.*

The time: World War II. The setting: Auschwitz, where a group of women prisoners, including conductor **Jane Alexander**, formed an orchestra to entertain their Nazi captors—and stave off death. Alexander cap-tured an Emmy, as did **Vanessa Redgrave** (bareheaded, third row left); playwright Arthur Miller won for scripting for the docudrama, and *Playing for Time* was named best dramatic special.

In 1961, Clarence Earl Gideon of Florida stood trial without a lawyer because he couldn't afford one. His appeal, based on the 14th Amendment's right to "due process," led to a landmark Supreme Court ruling guaranteeing all defendants counsel. The docudrama *Gideon's Trumpet* was based on a book by Anthony Lewis; star **Henry Fonda**, 74, would make one more movie—his Oscar-winning *On Golden Pond*—before his death in 1982.

Refereeing arm-wrassling matches was as good as it got in Cowtown, but at least *Flo* was back in Texas. This *Alice* spin-off began with **Polly Holliday** quitting Mel's Diner after four years and finding a shuttered cafe in her hometown—which she bought quicker than you can say "Kiss my grits." **Geoffrey Lewis** (right) played her bartender.

• • • • • • • • • •

LARRY HAGMAN

Whose series answered the question of "Who Shot J.R.?" in television's most-watched hour to date, on the shenanigans at South Fork:

"Everybody says, 'What's the purpose of the show?' The purpose is to entertain. I'm not sure *Dallas* will be remembered as long as Shakespeare, Shaw, or Ibsen—but it will sure make a hell of a lot more money than they did."

1981

President Reagan survives when shot by John Hinckley, 25, in Washington, D.C. Pope John Paul II survives when shot by Turkish hitman Mehmet Ali Agca, 23, at the Vatican. But Anwar Sadat, 63, does not when Egyptian soldiers parading in Cairo, angered by his peace talks with Israel, strafe the reviewing stand with grenades and gunfire. Sandra Day O'Connor, 51, is the first woman to sit on the U.S. Supreme Court.

Premiering series: *Dynasty* (ABC); *Entertainment Tonight* (SYND); *Falcon Crest* (CBS); *Gimme a Break!* (NBC); *Hill Street Blues* (NBC); *The People's Court* (with Judge Wapner); (SYND); *Simon & Simon* (CBS).

Movies: *Atlantic City*; *Chariots of Fire* (Oscar); Uys's *The Gods Must Be Crazy*; *The Road Warrior (Mad Max II)*; *On Golden Pond*; *Raiders of the Lost Ark*; *Reds*.

Songs: "Bette Davis Eyes" (Kim Carnes); "9 to 5" (Dolly Parton); "Physical" (Olivia Newton-John); "Queen of Hearts" (Juice Newton); "Private Eyes" (Daryl Hall and John Oates); "Woman" (John Lennon).

Books: *Gorky Park* (Martin Cruz Smith); *A Light in the Attic* (Shel Silverstein); *The White Hotel* (D.M. Thomas).

Died: actor William Holden, 63; boxer Joe Louis, 66; reggae's Bob Marley, 36; actress Natalie Wood, 45.

Debuts: AIDS (identified as a distinct disease of the immune system); IBM PC; MTV; Rubik's Cube.

Rope wasn't the only tie that bound **Jameson Parker** (near right) and **Gerald McRaney** in *Simon & Simon*: the San Diego–based private eyes they portrayed were also odd-couple brothers. The series was a midyear replacement that, in its first three (of six) full seasons, never ranked lower than No. 7 in the ratings.

Set in Northern California's wine country, *Falcon Crest* marked the primetime return of **Jane Wyman,** 65 (in the very same year her first husband entered the White House). The star, seated, portrayed a vinegary vintner battling nephew **Robert Foxworth** (second row, right) for control of the family business. The sour grapes would runneth over for nine years, six of which the series spent in Nielsen's Top 25.

Outside the Hilton Hotel in Washington, D.C., **Ronald Reagan** was about to step into his armored limousine when he suddenly clutched his side. The fourth U.S. president hit by an assassin's bullet, he would be the first to survive. Gunman John Hinckley, 25—who also wounded a D.C. cop, a secret serviceman, and Press Secretary James Brady—would be found not guilty by reason of insanity and institutionalized.

At 61, **Mickey Rooney** finally won an Emmy for his portrayal of a mentally retarded man coping with his move to a group home from the institution where he had spent most of his life. The success of *Bill*, which was based on a true story, inspired the 1982 sequel *Bill: On His Own*, also starring Rooney.

An estimated worldwide audience of 750 million witnessed, live, the marriage in London of Lady **Diana Frances Spencer**, 20, to **Charles Philip Arthur George**, 32 (who in addition to being Prince of Wales bore the titles Earl of Chester, Duke of Cornwall, Duke of Rothesay, Earl of Carrick, Baron of Renfrew, Lord of the Isles, and Grand Steward of Scotland).

In 1977, an American neo-Nazi group requested a permit to demonstrate in a heavily Jewish Chicago suburb. Reluctantly supporting them: a Jewish ACLU lawyer who saw it as a First Amendment free speech issue. The telemovie *Skokie* dramatized the controversy, with **John Rubenstein** (right) portraying the lawyer and **Danny Kaye** an angry town resident who during World War II had survived a German death camp.

• • • • • • • • • •

WALTER CRONKITE

Who passed the CBS News anchor to Dan Rather, on his signature sign-off, "And that's the way it is...":

"I came up with it when the *Evening News* went to a half hour in 1963. Recited with humor or sadness or irony, [it was] a six-word commentary on life's foibles. The public seemed to embrace it as they had Lowell Thomas's 'So long until tomorrow' and Ed Murrow's 'Good night and good luck.'"

A rgentina seizes the Falklands, offshore islands ruled by Britain since 1833, but withdraws after a bloody six-week sea-and-air war in the South Atlantic. Soviet leader Leonid Brezhnev dies at 75; replacing him is ex-KGB head Yuri Andropov, 68. Israel invades Lebanon and is followed by U.S. Marines sent in to act as peacekeepers.

Premiering series : *Cagney & Lacey* (CBS); *Cheers* (NBC); *Family Ties* (NBC); *Knight Rider* (NBC); *Newhart* (CBS); *Remington Steele* (NBC); *St. Elsewhere* (NBC); *Silver Spoons* (NBC); *Square Pegs* (CBS).

Movies: *Blade Runner*; Petersen's *Das Boot*; *E.T. the Extra-Terrestrial*; *48 HRS*; *Gandhi* (Oscar); *Tootsie*; *Victor/Victoria*.

Songs: "Abracadabra" (The Steve Miller Band); "Eye of the Tiger" (Survivor); "Gloria" (Laura Branigan); "Hurts So Good" (John Cougar); "Rosanna" (Toto); "Shake It Up" (The Cars).

Books: *The Color Purple* (Alice Walker); *In Search of Excellence* (Thomas Peters and Robert Waterman); *Jane Fonda's Workout Book* (Jane Fonda); *The Soul of a New Machine* (Tracy Kidder).

Died: comic John Belushi, 33; actress Ingrid Bergman, 67; actor Henry Fonda, 77; pianist Glenn Gould, 50; Princess Grace of Monaco, 52; baseball's Satchel Paige, 75.

Debuts: artificial heart (recipient Barney Clark, 61, survives 112 days); *USA Today*; Pac-Man arcade game.

In the same year the Equal Rights Amendment died short of ratification, *Cagney & Lacey* (**Sharon Gless**, in tan coat, and **Tyne Daly**) proved that women had the right stuff to be NYPD officers. The police drama would survive rocky initial ratings to run seven seasons. Of its 10 Emmys, Daly and Gless would win six for best actress.

Having defected from the Soviet Union in 1974 to join the American Ballet Theatre, **Mikhail Baryshnikov** made his movie debut three years later in *The Turning Point* with Anne Bancroft and Shirley MacLaine. At 34, the dancer starred in the primetime special *Baryshnikov in Hollywood*, with *pas de deux*-mate **Bernadette Peters** and Gene Wilder.

The battle over a design to remember America's Vietnam dead had been less bloody —but no less controversial—than the war itself. The quarreling stopped when President Ronald Reagan formally unveiled the Vietnam Veterans Memorial in Washington, D.C. The twin 247-foot-long black granite walls designed by Yale architecture student Maya Lin, incised with 57,939 names (252 would later be added), moved both hawks and doves to tears.

In the telemovie *A Piano for Mrs. Cimino*, **Bette Davis,** 74, played a freshly widowed septuagenarian whose grief is mistaken by relatives for senility. Involuntarily committed to a home, she regains her emotional balance with the aid of new friend **Keenan Wynn** and mounts a legal fight to get back not only her possessions but also her life.

"The Catch" by San Francisco 49er **Dwight Clark** of a desperation Joe Montana pass ranks with Pittsburgh Steeler Franco Harris's 1972 "Immaculate Reception" as the most timely touchdown grab in NFL history. Clark's last-second acrobatics in the NFC title game propelled his team past Dallas, 28–27, and into Super Bowl XVI.

Returning to primetime after a four-year hiatus, **Bob Newhart** became a dilettante Vermont innkeeper in *Newhart*. His wife was played by Mary Frann and the local yokels by (from left) **Tom Poston**, **Peter Scolari**, **William Sanderson**, **Tony Papenfuss**, and **John Volstad.** The sitcom would run eight years, one more than Newhart's first.

• • • • • • • • • •

ED BRADLEY

Who, during 11 years at CBS News, had patrolled beats ranging from the Vietnam War to the White House, on his new assignment, 60 Minutes:

"When I get to the Pearly Gates and St. Peter asks me what I've done to gain entry, I'll reply, 'Have you seen my Lena Horne profile?'"

1983

Korean Airlines Flight 007 flies over sensitive military installations deep in Soviet airspace and is shot down by Su-15 fighters; 269 die. A terrorist truck-bomb demolishes a U.S. barrack in Beirut, Lebanon, killing 241 sleeping Marines. Two days later President Reagan sends American troops to oust a leftist regime on the Caribbean isle of Grenada (pop. 90,000). After 132 years the U.S. loses yachting's America's Cup (to Australia).

Premiering series: *The A Team* (NBC); *Hotel* (ABC); *Scarecrow and Mrs. King* (CBS); *Webster* (ABC); *The Yellow Rose* (NBC).

Movies: *The Big Chill*; *Flashdance*; *Local Hero*; *Tender Mercies*; *Terms of Endearment* (Oscar); *Trading Places*; *WarGames*.

Songs: "Billie Jean" (Michael Jackson); "Do You Really Want to Hurt Me" (Culture Club); "Down Under" (Men at Work); "Every Breath You Take" (The Police); "Let's Dance" (David Bowie); "Sweet Dreams (Are Made of This)" (Eurythmics); "Uptown Girl" (Billy Joel).

Books: *Ironweed* (William Kennedy); *Modern Times* (Paul Johnson); *The Name of the Rose* (Umberto Eco).

Died: exiled Filipino leader Benigno Aquino, 50 (by assassination, on returning to Manila); singer Karen Carpenter, 32; TV host Arthur Godfrey, 79.

Debuts: Cabbage Patch Doll; Trivial Pursuit; aspartame-sweetened foods; junk bonds (invented by Michael Milken, 37).

As **Charlton Heston** (near right) parted a sea of bystanders, cop **Brad Davis** kept serving up shots of southern discomfort in the miniseries *Chiefs*. Other stars of the six-hour drama, about a Dixie town that harbors a mass murderer for three generations: Wayne Rogers, Tess Harper, Stephen Collins, Billy Dee Williams, and Keith Carradine.

What more unobtrusive aide could a spy have than a soccer mom? In *Scarecrow and Mrs. King*, **Bruce Boxleitner** played a homegrown Bond with the goofy cover name and **Kate Jackson** a suburban divorcée with a taste for skullduggery. Their series would make the Top 25 two of its four seasons on-air.

First American woman to orbit Earth: **Sally Ride,** one of five astronauts aboard the shuttle *Challenger*. During the six-day mission the 32-year-old physicist helped test the craft's brand-new robotic arm. She was the second woman in space, after Valentina Tereshkova of the U.S.S.R. in 1963.

Svengali marked the return to primetime of recent Yale grad **Jodie Foster,** 23 (who as a child had appeared in such series as *The Courtship of Eddie's Father* and *Paper Moon*). Her role: an aspiring rock singer in thrall to insanely possessive mentor **Peter O'Toole.** The telemovie was based on the novel by George du Maurier.

213

March rarely saw more madness than North Carolina State basketball coach **Jim Valvano**'s wild charge onto the court. His underdog Wolfpack had just edged the University of Houston, 54–52, on Lorenzo Charles's bucket at the final buzzer, to win the NCAA title.

In *The Scarlet and the Black*, **Gregory Peck**, 67, portrayed Monsignor Hugh O'Flaherty, a Vatican official who, during World War II, helped conceal some 4,000 escaped Allied POWs from the Nazi forces occupying Rome. The three-hour telemovie costarred Christopher Plummer as an SS colonel and John Gielgud as Pope Pius XII.

R onald Reagan defeats Walter F. Mondale to retain the presidency. When Sikhs occupy a temple in Amritsar, India, Indira Gandhi sends in troops who slay 400. Five months later the prime minister, 66, is shot dead by two Sikh bodyguards. A third Indian catastrophe: leaking toxic gas at a Union Carbide plant in Bhopal kills 3,500. The U.S.S.R. and 13 allies boycott the L.A. Olympics.

Premiering series : *Airwolf* (CBS); *The Cosby Show* (NBC); *Hunter* (NBC); *Kate & Allie* (CBS); *Miami Vice* (NBC); *Mike Hammer* (CBS); *Muppet Babies* (CBS); *Murder, She Wrote* (CBS); *Night Court* (NBC); *Punky Brewster* (NBC); *Who's the Boss?* (ABC)

Movies: *Amadeus* (Oscar); *Beverly Hills Cop*; *Ghostbusters*; *A Passage to India*; *Romancing the Stone*; *Splash*; *The Terminator*.

Songs: "Dancing in the Dark" (Bruce Springsteen); "Girls Just Want to Have Fun" (Cyndi Lauper); "Jump (For My Love)" (The Pointer Sisters); "Like a Virgin" (Madonna); "Wake Me Up Before You Go-Go" (Wham!); "When Doves Cry" (Prince).

Books: *The Hunt for Red October* (Tom Clancy); *Iacocca* (Lee Iacocca); *Neuromancer* (William Gibson).

Died: photographer Ansel Adams, 82; singer Marvin Gaye, 44 (shot by his father); director François Truffaut, 52.

In *George Washington*, 38-year-old **Barry Bostwick** (in tricorn, center) portrayed the young colonial surveyor who became a warrior and then America's first president. The success of the eight-hour miniseries would lead to a four-hour sequel; 1986's *George Washington: The Forging of a Nation*, again starring Bostwick, focused on Washington's two terms in office.

Was there ever a line more tailored for **George C. Scott** than "Bah, humbug!"? It came with the role of Ebenezer Scrooge, whom the actor portrayed in an adaptation of the 1843 Charles Dickens classic, *A Christmas Carol*. Scott's supporting cast included **Edward Woodward** as Christmas Present, as well as Nigel Davenport, David Warner, and Roger Rees.

Geraldine Ferraro became the first woman to run on a major-party ticket when Democratic presidential nominee Walter Mondale named her his choice for vice president. The New York congresswoman, 49, was also the first to lose. Despite Ferraro's debate performance against incumbent **George Bush,** the only state her team carried was Mondale's native Minnesota.

Pals since high school, *Kate & Allie* ended up divorced Manhattanites who decided to pool both finances and kids. **Susan Saint James** (right) and **Jane Curtin** headed the household, which included (from left) **Allison Smith**, **Frederick Koehler**, and **Ari Meyers**. The sitcom would win three Emmys during its five seasons, two of them by Curtin.

Terrible Joe Moran found ex-prizefighter **James Cagney** reduced to a wheelchair and dependent on longtime pal **Art Carney**. Entering their quiet lives: Moran's granddaughter, a troubled young woman who led with her chin (Ellen Barkin). The telemovie, for which Carney, 66, won his first dramatic Emmy after four for comedy, marked the final performance by the 84-year-old Cagney, who would die in 1986.

What was **Buddy Hackett** really trying to say to **Sheree North** (as other guest stars and **Angela Lansbury** listened in)? The keen powers of observation that enabled Lansbury's mystery novelist to construct bestsellers also helped her solve *Murder,* *She Wrote*'s weekly crime. The whodunnit would be a perennial Nielsen hit (spending three of its 12 years in the Top 5 plus six more in the Top 10) and win Lansbury induction into the Television Hall of Fame.

In
Their
Own
Words

• • • • • • • •

SUSAN SAINT JAMES

On the relationship between the protagonists of her new sitcom:

"Kate and Allie didn't plan [to live together], but divorce has hit hard everywhere. Their friendship sustains them. Even if one of us married, we could live upstairs from one another— Ethel and Lucy were neighbors and it worked."

At 54, Mikhail Gorbachev is the U.S.S.R.'s youngest leader since Stalin. French spies blow up a Greenpeace ship in New Zealand to keep it from interfering with a nuclear test in the Pacific. Explorer Robert Ballard finds the wreck of *Titanic*. Pete Rose's 4,192nd hit, a single, breaks Ty Cobb's mark.

Premiering series: *The Equalizer* (CBS); *The Golden Girls* (NBC); *Growing Pains* (ABC); *Larry King Live!* (CNN); *MacGyver* (ABC); *Mr. Belvedere* (ABC); *Moonlighting* (ABC); *Spenser: For Hire* (ABC).

Movies: *Back to the Future*; *Kiss of the Spider Woman*; *A Nightmare on Elm Street*; *Out of Africa* (Oscar); *Prizzi's Honor*; *Rambo: First Blood Part II*; Lanzmann's *Shoah*.

Songs: "The Boys of Summer" (Don Henley); "Close to Me" (The Cure); "Money for Nothing" (Dire Straits); "Shout" (Tears for Fears); "Smooth Operator" (Sade); "Take on Me" (a-ha); "We Are the World" (USA for Africa).

Books: *Common Ground* (J. Anthony Lukas); *Lake Wobegon Days* (Garrison Keillor); *Yeager* (Chuck Yeager).

Died: designer Laura Ashley, 60; zoologist Dian Fossey, 53 (murdered in Rwanda); actor Rock Hudson, 59 (of AIDS); baseball's Roger Maris, 51; singer Rick Nelson, 45; comic Phil Silvers, 74.

Debuts: ozone "hole" over Antarctica (described by British scientists); compact discs; Home Shopping Network; New Coke.

The miniseries *Space* ran 13 hours over five consecutive nights—but then, the epic James Michener novel from which it was drawn opened in Hitler's Germany and ended with America's moon landings. Principal cast members: James Garner, Susan Anspach, Bruce Dern, Blair Brown, Beau Bridges, Melinda Dillon, and Harry Hamlin.

Emmy winners **Dustin Hoffman** and **John Malkovich** (right) exchanged venomous salvos in front of **Ron Liebman** in a prime-time staging of *Death of a Salesman*. The previous year Hoffman, in his first role since *Tootsie*, had portrayed Willy Loman on Broadway in a Tony-winning revival of the 1949 Arthur Miller classic. Life after *Death* would not prove as rewarding; his next turn was opposite Warren Beatty in *Ishtar*.

Rock Hudson's increasing gauntness was noted by reporters covering a joint appearance with longtime pal **Doris Day** and also by the cast of *Dynasty,* on which he characteristically played a Lothario. He finally became the first Hollywood star to publicly confirm having contracted AIDS. Ten weeks later Hudson was dead, at age 59.

Eleven years after the conclusion of her last CBS sitcom, *Here's Lucy,* **Lucille Ball** played it straight as a bag lady in the telemovie *Stone Pillow.* The actress, 74, endured location filming on the streets of New York to portray a woman whose once-cozy life has deteriorated into eating out of dumpsters and sleeping in doorways. Daphne Zuniga was the young social worker trying to coax her client to a shelter.

Kirk Douglas rarely felt in the holiday spirit in *Amos*. Not only was his 78-year-old character penned up in a home but, thanks to cuckoo's-nest nurse **Elizabeth Montgomery**, patients never got well enough to leave. The telemovie was a rare network appearance by the 66-year-old Douglas, whose other costars were Ray Walston, Dorothy McGuire, and Pat Morita.

If his upper lip seemed a bit stiff and his accent a trifle plummy for an American spy turned Manhattan-based hired gun, it was because *The Equalizer*'s **Edward Woodward** hailed from England. The actor, 55, had starred in such sleepers as *The Wicker Man* and *Breaker Morant* before playing a mercenary who aided only the deserving; the hour-long drama would run four seasons.

TYNE DALY

Winner of her third straight Emmy for Cagney & Lacey, on one motif of the series:

"No breakthrough stuff like *Hill Street Blues*, just two lady cops in the john talking it over instead of two guys. Women are not by nature in competition. They are not innately bitchy and trying to get each other's husband. They are in fact wonderful cooperators and capable of friend-ships that are deep and mutually satisfying."

The shuttle *Challenger* explodes, killing seven. In Chernobyl, the Ukraine, fire guts a Soviet nuclear plant and subjects northern Europe to radioactive fallout. Secret White House arms deals (with Iran and with Nicaragua's contras) become public. *Pioneer 10*, launched by NASA in 1972, is the first man-made object to leave the solar system.

Premiering series: *ALF* (NBC); *Amen* (NBC); *Designing Women* (CBS); *Head of the Class* (ABC); *L.A. Law* (NBC); *Matlock* (NBC); *My Sister Sam* (CBS); *The Oprah Winfrey Show* (SYND); *Pee-wee's Playhouse* (CBS); *Perfect Strangers* (ABC).

Movies: *Aliens*; Rademaker's *The Assault*; *Blue Velvet*; *"Crocodile" Dundee*; *Down and Out in Beverly Hills*; *Platoon* (Oscar); *Top Gun*.

Songs: "Addicted to Love" (Robert Palmer); "Dancing on the Ceiling" (Lionel Richie); "Higher Love" (Steve Winwood); "How Will I Know" (Whitney Houston); "Walk Like an Egyptian" (The Bangles); "West End Girls" (The Pet Shop Boys).

Books: *Fatherhood* (Bill Cosby); *The Handmaid's Tale* (Margaret Atwood); *Maus* (Art Spiegelman).

Died: writer Jorge Luis Borges, 86; actor Cary Grant, 81; writer Bernard Malamud, 72; painter Georgia O'Keeffe, 98.

Debuts: RU-486 (the "morning-after" abortion pill); Nintendo video games.

It was NASA's 25th shuttle mission and *Challenger*'s 10th flight since joining the fleet in 1983. But 74 seconds after liftoff, an O-ring in the right booster rocket ruptured. The explosion left at least four of the seven astronauts alive and conscious; none, though, survived the nine-mile fall into the Atlantic. The catastrophe would ground America's manned space program for 30 months.

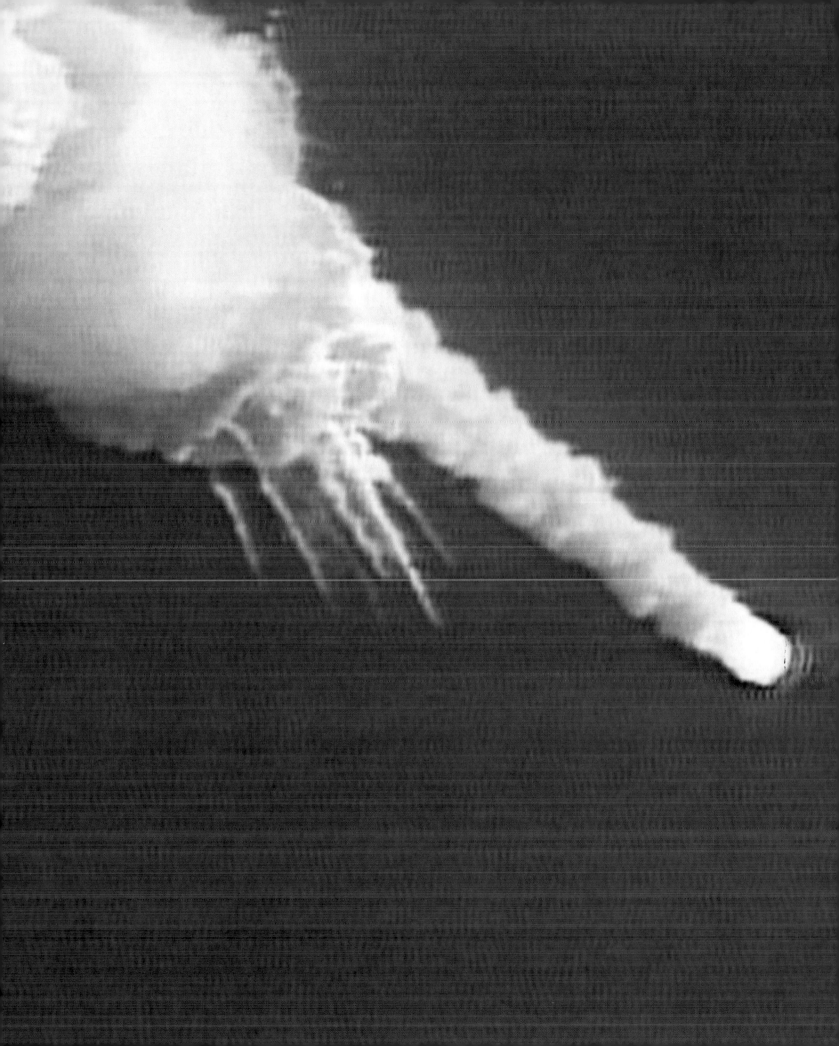

Having anchored the hit miniseries
Shogun, The Thorn Birds, and *Wallenberg,*
Richard Chamberlain (mounted, left)
portrayed John Frémont in the seven-
hour *Dream West.* The controversial 19th-
century figure mapped the Oregon Trail,
helped wrest California from Mexico, was
stripped of his Civil War command by
Lincoln, and held public office in both the
state of California and the Arizona territory.

After the unexpected success of the movie *Pee-wee's Big Adventure*, **Paul Reubens**, 34, brought his manic manchild to Saturday morning's *Pee-wee's Playhouse*. (One Fun Club regular: S. Epatha Merkerson, who went on to primetime's *Law & Order*.) Reubens's 1991 arrest at a XXX-cinema would end his kiddie show but not his career. Among his later gigs: *Batman Returns* and a role in CBS's *Murphy Brown*.

Pam Dawber (near left) was just beginning to blossom as a San Francisco–based freelance photographer when her doorbell rang: kid sib **Rebecca Schaeffer** needed a place to crash. *My Sister Sam* placed 21st in the Nielsens its first year but tumbled badly after a schedule switch. In 1989, after the sitcom's cancellation, Schaeffer, then 21, would be slain by a fan-turned-stalker.

Nine CBS News correspondents and 18 camera crews spent an entire weekend blanketing New York City and its suburbs in search of those who used and those who sold crack, the cheap street form of cocaine. The raw power of their two-hour primetime report, *48 Hours on Crack Street*, would lead to *48 Hours*, the weekly series that similarly explores a single topic in depth.

Whether recommending the right throw rug or pulling the rug out from under one another, the *Designing Women* who ran an Atlanta interior-decorating firm—**Annie Potts** (left), **Dixie Carter**, **Jean Smart**, and **Delta Burke**—were rarely at a loss for wisecracks. The sitcom would run seven seasons, placing as high as No. 6.

In
Their
Own
Words

· · · · · · · · · ·

KEN VENTURI

The 1964 winner of one of his sport's most hallowed events, the U.S. Open, on becoming CBS's golf analyst and Masters mainstay after leaving the PGA tour:

"Would I be doing television if I hadn't won the Open? I don't know. Winning the Open gave everything else I did credibility."

Testifying before Congress, Marine Lt. Col. Oliver North, 43, blames his role in the Iran–contra arms deals on orders from his bosses (including late CIA head William Casey). Sex scandals derail the presidential bid of Democrat Gary Hart and the teleministry of Jim Bakker. On Black Monday, the Dow Jones plummets 508 points, or 20 percent.

Premiering series: *Beauty and the Beast* (CBS); *The Bold and the Beautiful* (CBS); *The Days and Nights of Molly Dodd* (NBC); *Full House* (ABC); *Jake and the Fatman* (CBS); *Married...with Children* (FOX); *Star Trek: The Next Generation* (SYND); *thirtysomething* (ABC); *Tour of Duty* (CBS); *Wiseguy* (CBS).

Movies: Axel's *Babette's Feast*; *Dirty Dancing*; *Fatal Attraction*; *The Last Emperor* (Oscar); *Moonstruck*; *The Untouchables*.

Songs: "Alone" (Heart); "Faith" (George Michael); "Graceland" (Paul Simon); "I Still Haven't Found What I'm Looking For" (U2); "I Think We're Alone Now" (Tiffany); "Luka" (Suzanne Vega); "Shake Your Love" (Debbie Gibson).

Books: *And the Band Played On* (Randy Shilts); *Beloved* (Toni Morrison); *The Closing of the American Mind* (Allan Bloom); *Presumed Innocent* (Scott Turow).

Died: dancer Fred Astaire, 88; comic Jackie Gleason, 68; director John Huston, 81; pianist (Wladziu Valentino "Lee") Liberace, 68; guitarist Andrés Segovia, 94; pop artist Andy Warhol, 56.

Debuts: Prozac; Bud Light.

Glasnost, Mikhail Gorbachev's policy of openness, sent nine CBS News correspondents, led by **Ed Bradley, Diane Sawyer,** and **Dan Rather**, to Russia to film *The Soviet Union—Seven Days in May*. Highlights of the two-hour primetime special: interviews with average citizens; a heavy-metal concert in Vilnius; a drug bust in the republic of Georgia; and Sawyer's interview with Politburo up-and-comer Boris Yeltsin.

Rutger Hauer led the sprint to freedom in
Escape from Sobibor, based on a 1943
rebellion at Nazi-run death camps in Poland.
The three-hour telemovie costarred Alan Arkin
and Joanna Pacula. Of the 600-plus inmates
participating in the meticulously planned
breakout, over half made it to safety—the
largest mass escape in World War II history.

Wiseguy was the federal undercover agent played by **Ken Wahl** (with guest star **Fred Thompson**, who went legit in 1994 when elected a U.S. Senator from Tennessee). The innovative series featured cases requiring up to 10 hour-long episodes, or "arcs," to crack. Among those giving memorable turns as villains during its three-season run: Ray Sharkey, Kevin Spacey, and Stanley Tucci.

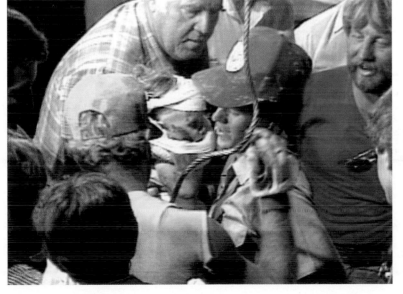

A primetime audience saw 18-month-old **Jessica McClure** finally hauled to safety after 58 hours in an abandoned Texas well. (She had been wedged in a section of shaft too narrow for any of the 450 rescue workers to fit.) Lost in the excitement over the toddler's retrieval: the uncapped well was situated in the backyard of her aunt's unlicensed day-care center.

Appearing before a House panel probing Iran-contra, Marine Lt. Col. **Oliver North**, 43, defiantly admitted flouting several congressional bans. While serving as a National Security Council aide, he had helped arrange the sale of arms to the Ayatollah Khomeini and then channel the illicit profits to Nicaragua's rightist rebels. His defense: "authority from my superiors," including Ronald Reagan —a claim heatedly denied by the president.

Unlike **Ron Perlman, Linda Hamilton** never had a bad hair day on *Beauty and the Beast*. She played a New York lawyer beaten and left to die, he a genetically challenged denizen of a secret underground city who nursed her back to health and then joined her fight against crime. Hamilton would leave the series in 1989 to prep for *Terminator 2*, but not before testing her savior's DNA. Happily, the child she bore him was indisputably humanoid.

In
Their
Own
Words

• • • • • • • • •

ANDY ROONEY

An Emmy-winning news writer who in 1981 began contributing commentaries to 60 Minutes, on a fear voiced by a legendary CBS journalist during television's infancy:

"Ed Murrow need not have worried. It's been better than wires and lights in a box."

George H.W. Bush defeats Michael S. Dukakis for the presidency. The Soviet Union withdraws from Afghanistan after eight and a half years and 16,000 dead. In the Persian Gulf, the U.S. warship *Vincennes* shoots down a civilian Iranian jetliner, killing 290. Six months later a terrorist bomb destroys Pan Am Flight 103, killing 259 and 11 residents of Lockerbie, Scotland. Steffi Graf, 19, wins tennis's Grand Slam for women.

Premiering series: *China Beach* (ABC); *Dear John...* (NBC); *Empty Nest* (NBC); *48 Hours* (CBS); *In the Heat of the Night* (NBC); *Murphy Brown* (CBS); *Paradise* (CBS); *Roseanne* (ABC); *The Wonder Years* (ABC).

Movies: *Big*; *Bull Durham*; *Die Hard*; *Married to the Mob*; *Rain Man* (Oscar); *Who Framed Roger Rabbit*; Almodovar's *Women on the Verge of a Nervous Breakdown*.

Songs: "Don't Worry Be Happy" (Bobby McFerrin); "Fast Car" (Tracy Chapman); "Look Away" (Chicago); "Need You Tonight" (INXS); "Red Red Wine" (UB40); "Sweet Child o' Mine" (Guns n' Roses).

Books: *A Brief History of Time* (Stephen Hawking); *The Making of the Atomic Bomb* (Richard Rhodes); *The Satanic Verses* (Salman Rushdie).

Died: physicist Richard Feynman, 69; writer Robert Heinlein, 80; environmentalist Chico Mendes, 44; rock's Roy Orbison, 52.

Debuts: Energizer Bunny; Super Mario Brothers (from Nintendo).

CBS gained another public affairs program—sort of—with the premiere of *Murphy Brown,* a sitcom set in the Washington, D.C., offices of the fictional newsmagazine show *F.Y.I.* **Candice Bergen**, 42, portrayed a driven telejournalist; heading the supporting cast were (from near right) **Charles Kimbrough**, **Joe Regalbuto**, **Grant Shaud**, **Robert Pastorelli**, and **Faith Ford**. The series would win at least one Emmy for comedy in six of its first nine seasons.

It was reigning dogs the weekend *48 Hours* unleashed **Charles Kuralt** and CBS News colleagues Charles Osgood and Richard Schlesinger on Madison Square Garden, where the Westminster Kennel Club was staging its annual show for purebreds. The competition proved predictably nip-and-tuck.

It was reigning cats on Saturday mornings when *Garfield and Friends* got their own weekly series. Cartoonist Jim Davis's laid-back feline also purred his way to a third prime-time Emmy with the special *Garfield: Babes and Bullets.*

David Strathairn portrayed atom-bomb pioneer J. Robert Oppenheimer—here tinkering with "Fat Boy," which would devastate Hiroshima—in *Day One.* The Emmy-winning three-hour telemovie dramatized the Manhattan Project, America's top-secret WWII effort to beat Hitler's scientists to the ultimate weapon. Brian Dennehy and Michael Tucker costarred.

The charge of plastique, secreted in a portable tape recorder, was timed to go off when the London-to-New York flight was well out over the Atlantic. But because Pan Am Flight 103 was behind schedule, the detonation brought the 747 down atop the Scottish village of Lockerbie. By the time investigators identified the two bomb-planters, both had been granted safe haven by Libya's Muammar Quaddafi.

The L.A. rag biz provided double-stitched intrigue for *The Bold and the Beautiful*, a half-hour soap that retailed the woes of a family-run fashion shop. Among its principals: **Susan Flannery** and **John McCook** (seated) and, as their children, **Clayton Norcross** (left), **Ronn Moss**, and **Teri Ann Linn.** Actors who would beam down for a stint included Phyllis Diller, James Doohan, Tippi Hedren, Peter Brown, and Hunter Tylo.

DAN RATHER

CBS News anchor who also began hosting 48 Hours, *on print vs. broadcast journalism:*

"I don't believe you can be a fully informed person in our society and only watch tele-vision news. I also don't believe you can be fully informed and not watch."

When Chinese students occupy Beijing's Tiananmen Square to call for reforms, the government sends in troops; more than 300 die. Political protest has a happier ending in Europe, symbolized by the fall of the Berlin Wall. Poland, Hungary, and Czechoslovakia break from Moscow's orbit; Romanians oust and execute dictator Nicolae Ceausescu, 71. Another despot, Panama's Manuel Noriega, is caught by invading U.S. troops and flown to Miami to answer drug-trafficking charges.

Premiering series: *Anything But Love* (ABC); *Baywatch* (NBC); *Coach* (ABC); *Doctor, Doctor* (CBS); *Doogie Howser, M.D.* (ABC); *Family Matters* (ABC); *Father Dowling Mysteries* (NBC); *Life Goes On* (ABC); *Major Dad* (CBS); *Rescue 911* (CBS); *The Simpsons* (FOX).

Movies: *Batman*; *Bill and Ted's Excellent Adventure*; *Do the Right Thing*; *Driving Miss Daisy* (Oscar); *Drugstore Cowboy*; *My Left Foot*; *When Harry Met Sally*.

Songs: "Girl You Know It's True" (Milli Vanilli); "Love Shack" (The B-52s); "Miss You Much" (Janet Jackson); "Orinoco Flow (Sail Away)" (Enya); "She Drives Me Crazy" (Fine Young Cannibals).

Books: *Parting the Waters* (Taylor Branch); *The Joy Luck Club* (Amy Tan).

Died: comedienne Lucille Ball, 77; actress Bette Davis, 81; actor Laurence Olivier, 82; comic Gilda Radner, 42; Russian physicist/political reformer Andrei Sakharov, 68.

Debuts: Teenage Mutant Ninja Turtles.

Robert Duvall shared memories of an Old West that was fast vanishing with **Rick Schroder**, 19, in *Lonesome Dove*, a miniseries costarring Tommy Lee Jones. Based on a novel by Larry McMurtry, the nine-hour Nielsen blockbuster's exceptional supporting cast included Anjelica Huston, Robert Urich, Diane Lane, and Danny Glover. Schroder would also appear in 1993's seven-hour *Return to Lonesome Dove*.

Red Army troops watched for more than six weeks as college students from across China occupied Beijing's Tiananmen Square. Their demand: a government less corrupt and more democratic. With international media coverage growing—and demonstrations spreading to other major cities—China's leader, Deng Xiaoping, ordered the Square cleared. It was, at the cost of an estimated 300 lives.

Rescue 911 dramatized case histories from the files of emergency-service agencies around the nation. The hour-long series, hosted by **William Shatner**, featured staged versions of rescues performed by cops, fire-fighters, and paramedics, with real-life participants providing the narration. It would run seven seasons.

During World War II, after a murder in an American run POW camp in Colorado, small-town lawyer **Walter Matthau** is pressured into representing the German charged with the crime. *The Incident* costarred Peter Firth and Harry Morgan.

It was shabby, graffiti-smeared, and surprisingly smaller-than-life; yet for 28 years the Berlin Wall had thwarted East Germans from fleeing to the West. Its dismantling—unopposed by the regime that built it—would be a harbinger of European Communism's swift tumble into history's dustbin.

Gung-ho Marine **Gerald McRaney** lost his interest in barhopping when a journalist sent to profile him turned out to be an attractive widow (Shanna Reed). Though she was also a flaming liberal, the by-the-rules Leatherneck soon put bachelorhood behind him to become *Major Dad* to her three daughters. The sitcom would finish one of its four seasons in the Top 10.

ast and West Germany reunite. After 27 years in jail, Nelson Mandela, 71, is freed by South Africa. Angered by the amount of oil Kuwait is extracting from a shared reserve, Iraq's Saddam Hussein invades his Persian Gulf neighbor. Retired Michigan pathologist Jack Kevorkian aids an Alzheimer's sufferer to die, his first known assisted suicide.

Premiering series: *America's Funniest Home Videos* (ABC); *Beverly Hills 90210* (FOX); *Evening Shade* (CBS); *The Fresh Prince of Bel-Air* (NBC); *In Living Color* (FOX); *Law & Order* (NBC); *Northern Exposure* (CBS); *Seinfeld* (NBC); *Twin Peaks* (ABC); *Wings* (NBC).

Movies: *Dances with Wolves* (Oscar); *Edward Scissorhands*; *Ghost*; *Goodfellas*; *Home Alone*; Verhoeven's *The Nasty Girl*; *Pretty Woman*.

Songs: "Love Takes Time" (Mariah Carey); "Ice Ice Baby" (Vanilla Ice); "Nothing Compares 2 U" (Sinead O'Connor); "Pump Up the Jam" (Technotronic); "U Can't Touch This" (M.C. Hammer).

Books: *Darkness Visible* (William Styron); *The Firm* (John Grisham); *Possession* (A.S. Byatt); *Rabbit at Rest* (John Updike).

Died: singer Pearl Bailey, 72; actress Greta Garbo, 84; puppeteer Jim Henson, 53; cartoonist B. Kliban, 55; CBS founder William Paley, 89; rock's Del Shannon, 50; AIDS icon Ryan White, 18.

Debuts: General Motors's Saturn; implanted contraceptive (Norplant).

Members of his beloved bestiary were on best behavior (sort of) in *The Muppets Celebrate Jim Henson*. Sadly, their tribute to television's most influential puppeteer (*Sesame Street*, *The Muppet Show*, cable's *Fraggle Rock*) was posthumous. Six months earlier **Henson** had ignored flu-like symptoms, never suspecting it was a rare but treatable staph infection; he died three days later, at age 53.

Rob Morrow was expecting maybe Bullwinkle? In *Northern Exposure*, the actor played a New York–bred doctor repaying his med school scholarship with four years in an Alaskan hamlet. The aggressively off-beat series costarred Janine Turner, Barry Corbin, John Corbett, and a stag named Morty. In its five seasons, the show would place in the Top 16 three times and win a trio of Emmys, including one for best drama.

What led **Barbara Hershey** to pull a Lizzie Borden on her best friend? The actress won an Emmy for her portrayal of a repressed Texas housewife in *A Killing in a Small Town*, a telemovie based on a true case; Brian Dennehy and Hal Holbrook costarred.

During his glory days he busted past defenders; now, the high-school football coach played by **Burt Reynolds,** 54, was considerably easier to stop. Set in rural Arkansas, *Evening Shade* costarred Marilu Henner and **Michael Jeter** (with the walker). Both Reynolds and Jeter would win Emmys during the sitcom's four-year run.

Twenty-year-old **Gabriela Sabatini** of Argentina edged defending two-time champ Steffi Graf for the women's crown at the U.S. Open, an event telecast by CBS since 1968. The men's title went to first-time winner Pete Sampras, 19.

In *Common Ground*, **Jane Curtin** portrayed a South End widow with seven kids caught up in the racially divisive busing controversy that rocked Boston in the 1970s. The four-hour docudrama was based on the Pulitzer prize–winning book by J. Anthony Lukas; it costarred Richard Thomas, James Farentino, and C.C.H. Pounder.

● ● ● ● ● ● ● ● ●

BOB BARKER

Winner, at age 66, of his sixth Daytime Emmy for hosting The Price Is Right, *on the key to his network career, which began in 1956 with* Truth or Consequences:

"I help contestants to be funny, but I never make fun of them."

I n Operation Desert Storm, allied forces commanded by U.S. General Norman Schwarzkopf need 100 hours to rid Kuwait of Iraqi troops. The U.S.S.R. is dissolved, to be replaced by the 11-member Commonwealth of Independent States. The confirmation of Clarence Thomas to the Supreme Court is delayed by Senate hearings into charges he sexually harassed Anita Hill. LAPD officers are videotaped savaging an unarmed black motorist named Rodney King.

Premiering series: *Brooklyn Bridge* (CBS); *The Commish* (ABC); *Home Improvement* (ABC); *Sisters* (NBC).

Movies: *The Addams Family; Beauty and the Beast; City Slickers; The Commitments;* Salvatores's *Mediterraneo; The Silence of the Lambs* (Oscar); *Thelma & Louise.*

Songs: "Baby Baby" (Amy Grant); "(Everything I Do) I Do It for You" (Bryan Adams); "It's So Hard to Say Goodbye to Yesterday" (Boyz II Men); "Losing My Religion" (R.E.M.); "O.P.P." (Naughty by Nature); "Ropin' the Wind" (Garth Brooks).

Books: *Backlash* (Susan Faludi); *The Beauty Myth* (Naomi Wolf); *A Dangerous Woman* (Mary McGarry Morris).

Died: jazz's Miles Davis, 65; author Theodore (Dr. Seuss) Geisel, 87; automaker Soichiro Honda, 84; Polaroid inventor Edwin Land, 81; rock's Freddie Mercury, 45.

Debuts: Buckyballs (pure-carbon molecules with superconductivity potential).

Glenn Close portrayed a spinster who moved from New England to Kansas to become the mail-order bride of a widower with two youngsters (**Christopher Bell** and **Lexi Randall**) in *Sarah, Plain and Tall.* The telemovie, drawn from a novel by Patricia MacLachlan, costarred Christopher Walken. The cast would reunite in a 1993 sequel, *Skylark*.

In the four-hour docudrama *In a Child's Name*, **Valerie Bertinelli** (second from right) fought to prove that her murdered sister's husband committed the crime. Though convicted, he mounted a new legal challenge from behind bars: a custody battle for his son (and her nephew). Michael Ontkean costarred.

The traffic bust outside his North Hollywood home was so contentious that a plumbing-store manager grabbed his videocam. When the tape aired nationally, **Rodney King**, 25, would no longer be unknown. Nor would the LAPD officers who beat him; though acquitted of police brutality (a verdict that set off riots), two were convicted on federal charges of violating King's civil rights.

MAR. 3 1991

On *Brooklyn Bridge*, brothers **Danny Gerard** (far left) and **Matthew Louis Siegel** grew up at a time when the world champion Dodgers were still playing in Ebbets Field and Elvis had not yet played *The Ed Sullivan Show*. The nostalgic half-hour series was acclaimed by critics but would fail to find an audience during its two-season run.

Following a five-month buildup and a two-week aerial bombardment of Iraq, Desert Storm's ground attack needed just over four days to drive Saddam Hussein's army from Kuwait. The allied coalition's attempt to control the press drove some reporters to take risks in covering the Gulf War. Correspondent Bob Simon was one of four CBS Newsmen jailed by Iraq for 40 days before their safe release.

Considered an eyesore on Manhattan's posh Upper East Side, the homeless woman played by **Tyne Daly** in *Face of a Stranger* gained the sympathies of a socialite whom widowhood had left suddenly impoverished. Costar Gena Rowlands won an Emmy for portraying the telemovie's widow.

LESLEY STAHL

The newest 60 Minutes correspondent, on gender bias:

"I can honestly say that in my career I've never seen any against me because I'm a woman. I think if there is a prejudice in our business, it's against age rather than sex. My male counterparts worry as much about getting older and showing lines on their faces as we do."

Bill (William J.B.) Clinton defeats George Bush for the presidency; independent Ross Perot wins 19 percent of the vote. Sarajevo, host of the '84 Winter Games, is besieged in the civil war sundering the former Yugoslavia. Four white police officers are acquitted of beating black motorist Rodney King, triggering heavy rioting in South-Central Los Angeles. First non-U.S. major league baseball champs: the Toronto Blue Jays.

Premiering series: *Hearts Afire* (CBS); *Love and War* (CBS); *Mad About You* (NBC); *Melrose Place* (FOX); *Picket Fences* (CBS).

Movies: *Basic Instinct*; *The Crying Game*; *My Cousin Vinny*; Zhang's *The Story of Qiu Ju*; *Under Siege*; *Unforgiven* (Oscar); *Wayne's World*.

Songs: "Achy Breaky Heart" (Billy Ray Cyrus); "Baby Got Back" (Sir Mix-a-Lot); "I Will Always Love You" (Whitney Houston); "I'm Too Sexy" (Right Said Fred); "Jeremy" (Pearl Jam); "Smells Like Teen Spirit" (Nirvana); "Under the Bridge" (Red Hot Chili Peppers).

Books: *The Bridges of Madison County* (Robert James Waller); *Sabine's Notebook* (Nick Bantock); *Sex* (Madonna).

Died: actress Marlene Dietrich, 90; writer Alex Haley, 70; comic Sam Kinison, 38; pundit Eric Sevareid, 79; retailer Sam Walton, 74; Motown's Mary Wells, 49.

Debuts: Minnesota's Mall of America, the world's largest; nicotine patch.

Primetime novices **Bill Clinton**, 45, and **Hillary Rodham Clinton**, 44, were briefed on the *60 Minutes* drill by producer **Don Hewitt.** The couple had agreed to discuss the stories of infidelity threatening the Arkansas governor's front-running status in the upcoming Democratic primaries. Clinton neither confirmed nor denied one alleged liaison, but did own up to past problems in a marriage he and his wife insisted was now strong.

The rural-Wisconsin crimes occupying *Picket Fences* sheriff **Tom Skerritt** (with, clockwise, **Kathy Baker**, **Justin Shenk-arow**, **Adam Wylie**, and **Holly Marie Combs**) were, well, quirky. There was the woman who date-raped a guy, the midget who stole a circus elephant, the mayor who just burst into flames... Although the hour-long series would never crack Nielsen's Top 25, it won a dozen Emmys—including three by Baker—in its four seasons on-air.

Fowl play was par for the course on *Love & War*, in which gourmet chef **Susan Dey** and news columnist **Jay Thomas** often sautéed each other in front of waitress **Joanna Gleason** (while steaming romantically in private). The sitcom would run three seasons, the last two with Annie Potts as the new tocque who tickles Thomas's palate.

Sinatra needed all of five hours to reprise Old Blue Eyes's long and turbulent path from '40s crooner to Oscar-winning actor to Hollywood's Chairman of the Board. The miniseries, executive produced by daughter Tina, cast **Philip Casnoff** as Frank and, as Wives Nos. 1, 2, & 3, Gina Gershon (Nancy), Marcia Gay Harden (Ava Gardner), and Nina Siemaszko (Mia Farrow).

267

The real-life San Diego divorcée portrayed by **Meredith Baxter** in the telemovie *A Woman Scorned: The Betty Broderick Story* murdered her ex and his young second wife as they slept. Her defense—she was the victim of his emotional abuse—failed to sway a jury. But it drew high enough Nielsens to warrant a rapid sequel, *Her Final Fury: Betty Broderick the Last Chapter.*

Age Seven in America crisscrossed the country from Los Angeles to New York and from Nebraska to Georgia to elicit from kids born in the mid-1980s their hopes and fears. The primetime special, narrated by Meryl Streep, was produced by British director Michael Apted. His 1963 documentary *7 Up* similarly surveyed children in his homeland (whom he then revisited every seven years until completing *35 Up*).

· · · · · · · · ·

CANDICE BERGEN

Who gave birth to a campaign controversy and picked up Emmy No. 5, on her move from movies to primetime:

"When I agreed to do *Murphy* it really was not considered an appropriate choice. Not that I had a thriving film career, you understand, but you just didn't cross over. I was discouraged by everyone from doing it. It was like violating the caste system."

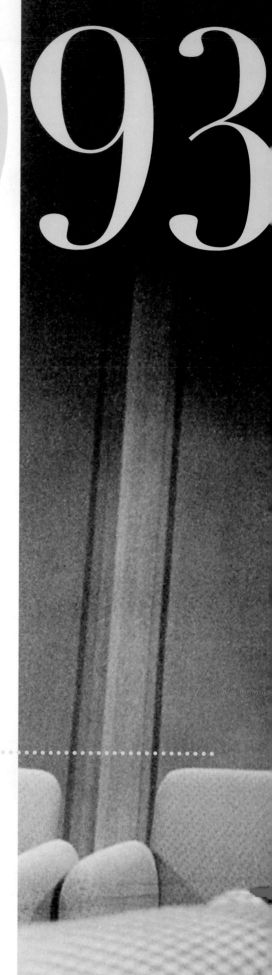

A bomb planted by Muslim extremists in New York's World Trade Center kills six and injures 1,000. Heartland floods cripple parts of nine states. Lorena Bobbitt slices husband John; a Steffi Graf fan stabs Monica Seles, 20, at a tennis tourney in Germany. After his dad's murder, Michael Jordan quits basketball at age 30, only to return in 1995.

Premiering series: *Beavis and Butt-head* (MTV); *Dave's World* (CBS); *Diagnosis Murder* (CBS); *Dr. Quinn, Medicine Woman* (CBS); *Frasier* (NBC); *Grace Under Fire* (ABC); *Homicide* (NBC); *Late Show with David Letterman* (CBS); *Lois and Clark: The New Adventures of Superman* (ABC); *The Nanny* (CBS); *NYPD Blue* (ABC); *Walker, Texas Ranger* (CBS); *The X-Files* (FOX).

Movies: *Dazed and Confused; The Fugitive; Jurassic Park; The Piano; Schindler's List* (Oscar); *Sleepless in Seattle.*

Songs: "All That She Wants" (Ace of Base); "Bad Boys" (Inner Circle); "I Get Around" (2Pac); "No Rain" (Blind Melon); "Two Princes" (Spin Doctors); "Whoomp! (There It Is)" (Tag Team).

Books: *The Celestine Prophecy* (James Redfield); *Private Parts* (Howard Stern).

Died: tennis's Arthur Ashe, 49; actor Raymond Burr, 76; director Federico Fellini, 73; actress Audrey Hepburn, 63; ballet's Rudolf Nureyev, 64; TV host Garry Moore, 78.

Debuts: U.S. Holocaust Museum in Washington, D.C.; proof, after 356 years, of Fermat's Last Theorem (by British mathematician Andrew Wiles).

Drew Barrymore was so thrilled by the new *Late Show with David Letterman* that she not only danced on the star's desk but also bared her, ummm, soul to him. Joining CBS after hosting NBC's post-midnight show for 11-plus years, the 46-year-old comedian would soon deliver what four decades of late-night vehicles (among them, talk shows built around Merv Griffin and Pat Sajak) never could: ratings.

Aural hygiene was just one good practice *Dr. Quinn, Medicine Woman* introduced to pioneer-era Colorado. The strong-willed Bostonian played by **Jane Seymour**, 42, went West to begin anew after her father's death. In the series's third season, she would marry costar Joe Lando's mountain man and add the role of little spouse on the prairie.

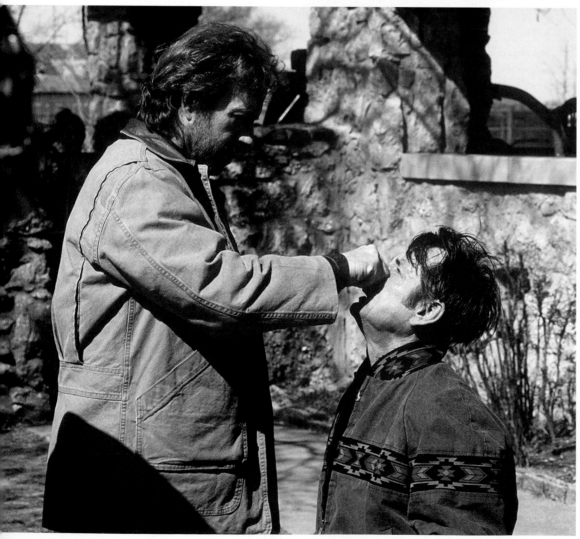

Policing primetime as *Walker, Texas Ranger,* **Chuck Norris** needed to interrogate slime-balls a bit more politely than in two dozen smash-mouth movies (*A Force of One, Silent Rage, Missing in Action*). No matter. Fans of the onetime karate champ, 54, would boot the show into the Top 20 by its third season.

The Nanny was an uncultured pearl from Queens charged with raising a veddy British widower's three kids in Manhattan. The most distinctive of star **Fran Drescher**'s comedic shtiks: her nasal bridge-and-tunnel honk. Costar Charles Shaughnessy played her boss, Daniel Davis the butler, and Nicholle Tom, Benjamin Salisbury, and Madeline Zima the children.

Halle Berry played a love child born in 1841 to the son of a plantation owner and his slave mistress in *Queen*, based on author Alex Haley's research into the life of his paternal grandmother. **Ossie Davis** portrayed one of Queen Haley's friends; the cast of the five-hour miniseries also included Jasmine Guy, Tim Daly, Ann-Margret, Martin Sheen, and Danny Glover.

Her first character named Rose earned **Bette Midler** an Oscar nomination (for her 1979 portrayal of a Janis Joplinesque rocker). Her second was not a druggie, just a stage mother who pushed her oldest daughter into burlesque. *Gypsy,* a three-hour adaptation of the Broadway musical, costarred Cynthia Gibb as the famed ecdysiast Gypsy Rose Lee, as well as Peter Riegert, Ed Asner, and Michael Jeter.

. . . .

DAVID LETTERMAN

*On his Top 10 tips
to aspiring comics:*

"Don't do it,
go into another
profession,
there's plenty of
competition,
don't bother me,
don't give me
something else to
worry about,
I'm having trouble
hanging on to my
job, I don't want
you breathing
down my neck,
we have enough
professionals
now providing all
the laughs this
country needs,
we don't want you,
stay home."

E xiled Haitian President Jean-Bertrand Aristide reclaims office after 15,000 U.S. troops oust a junta. Nelson Mandela wins the presidency of South Africa. Civil war splinters Rwanda. When baseball players strike, owners axe the World Series. Special prosecutor Ken Starr begins probing a 1980s Arkansas land deal made by then-governor Bill Clinton.

Premiering series: *Chicago Hope* (CBS); *Due South* (CBS); *ER* (NBC); *Friends* (NBC); *My So-Called Life* (ABC); *Party of Five* (FOX); *These Friends of Mine* (ABC); *Touched By An Angel* (CBS); *Under Suspicion* (CBS).

Movies: *Clerks*; *Dumb and Dumber*; *Forrest Gump* (Oscar); von Trier's *The Kingdom*; *The Lion King*; *Pulp Fiction*; *Speed*.

Songs: "All I Wanna Do" (Sheryl Crow); "Breathe Again" (Toni Braxton); "Come to My Window" (Melissa Etheridge); "Loser" (Beck); "Mmm Mmm Mmm Mmm" (Crash Test Dummies); "Stay (I Missed You)" (Lisa Loeb).

Books: *The Hot Zone* (Richard Preston); *How We Die* (Sherwin Nuland); *Midnight in the Garden of Good and Evil* (John Berendt).

Died: comedian John Candy, 43; rock's Kurt Cobain, 27 (a suicide); actor Burt Lancaster, 80; President Richard Nixon, 80; Jacqueline Onassis, 64; sprinter Wilma Rudolph, 54; journalist Randy Shilts, 42.

Debuts: the 31-mile Channel Tunnel linking England and France by rail; Chrysler Neon; Wonderbra; blue M&Ms.

Dan Jansen had stood poised to medal at the Winter Games of Calgary and Albertville, having dominated the international circuit, yet never finished better than fourth. The 1000-meter at Lillehammer was his last race in his final Olympics. Despite a wobble at the 600-meter mark, the 28-year-old speed skater raced home to win the gold.

In *Oldest Living Confederate Widow Tells All*, the titular character wed to Civil War vet **Donald Sutherland** was portrayed by two actresses: **Diane Lane** as his young bride and Anne Bancroft as his aging survivor. Cicely Tyson won a best-supporting Emmy for her role as a former slave in the four-hour miniseries, which was based on a novel by Alan Gurganus.

Arraigned only after a surreal L.A. freeway chase broadcast live around the globe, football star-turned-pitchman/actor **O.J. Simpson,** 46, pleaded not guilty to the knifing deaths of ex-wife No. 2, Nicole, and waiter Ron Goldman. His long-run trial would feature a plot (and a cast of lawyers, witnesses, jury members, and judge) worthy of a soap. Acquitted of the homicides, Simpson would keep custody of his kids but later lose a wrongful-death suit.

Celestial emissaries **Roma Downey** (right) and **John Dye** were still new at the business of ministering to troubled mortals, so supervisor **Della Reese** remained close at hand. Instead of wings, the *Touched By An Angel* trio journeyed down heaven's highways in a vintage red convertible. Whatever its means of locomotion, the series would soon ascend into the Top 10.

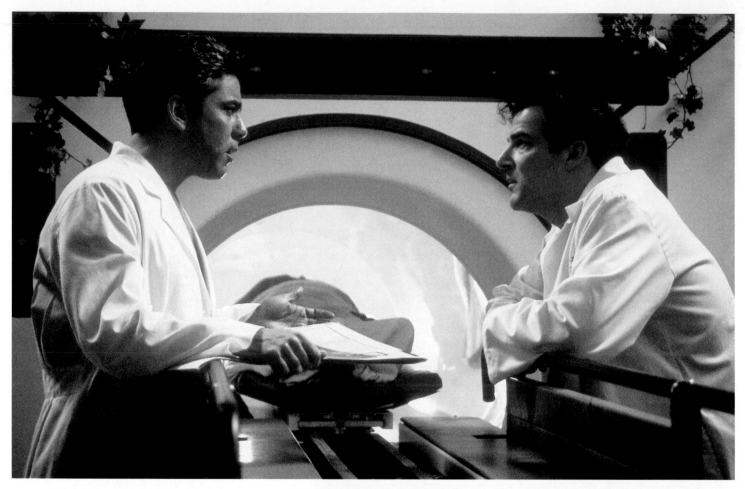

Let that hospital across town handle the quotidian cases; the medical center known as *Chicago Hope* specialized in procedures advanced enough to attract top-gun surgeons like **Adam Arkin** and **Mandy Patinkin**. The hour-long drama costarred Hector Elizondo, E.G. Marshall, and Roxanne Hart; the cast would later be joined by Christine Lahti.

When the mob muscled in on *Due South* guest star **Milton Berle**'s topless joint, the case went to an odd crime-fighting couple. **David Marciano** (left) was a Windy City native as intense as Starsky, **Paul Gross** a Canadian Mountie (on loan to the Chicago PD) as noble as Dudley Doright. The tongue-in-cheek police series would run two seasons.

A truck bomb parked by Timothy McVeigh destroys an Oklahoma City office building, killing 168. Six weeks after signing an accord granting Palestinians more autonomy, Prime Minister Yitzhak Rabin is assassinated by a right-wing Israeli zealot. Twelve die when a Japanese cult releases poison gas in Tokyo's subway. O.J. Simpson is acquitted of double murder. Cal Ripken Jr. breaks Lou Gehrig's record by playing his 2,131st straight game.

Premiering series: *Caroline in the City* (NBC); *Cybill* (CBS); *The Drew Carey Show* (ABC); *Hercules—The Legendary Journeys* (SYND); *The Naked Truth* (ABC); *NewsRadio* (NBC); *Xena: Warrior Princess* (SYND).

Movies: *Apollo 13; Babe; Braveheart* (Oscar); *Clueless; Get Shorty;* Radford's *Il Postino; While You Were Sleeping.*

Songs: "Happiness Is Slavery" (Nine Inch Nails); "Kiss from a Rose" (Seal); "Let Her Cry" (Hootie and the Blowfish); "Whose Bed Have Your Boots Been Under" (Shania Twain); "You Oughta Know" (Alanis Morissette).

Books: *Emotional Intelligence* (Daniel Goleman); *Longitude* (Dava Sobel).

Died: sportscaster Howard Cosell, 77; rock's Jerry Garcia, 53; baseball's Mickey Mantle, 63; virologist Jonas Salk, 80; Tejano diva Selena, 23 (shot dead by the ex-head of her fan club).

Debuts: Netscape, an Internet browser; Windows '95.

Self-love was not uncommon among Hollywood types, but **Cybill Shepherd**'s stand-in proved a bust even with unflappable pal **Christine Baranski**. On the sitcom *Cybill,* Shepherd, 45, played a onetime ingenue who found her career waning as her age kept waxing.

As **Sonia Braga** and **James Garner** discovered in *Streets of Laredo,* the rapidly vanishing Old West could still be plenty violent. The five-hour miniseries was based on Larry McMurtry's follow-up volume to his novel *Lonesome Dove.* Garner took over the role originated on television by Tommy Lee Jones; others in the powerhouse cast included Sissy Spacek, Sam Shepard, Ned Beatty, and Randy Quaid.

Mr. Wizard's low-keyed experiments had captivated Eisenhower-era youngsters; *Beakman's World* sped up the tempo to hook modern kids on science. **Paul Zaloom** played the title character of the show, which began on cable in 1992. When not wearing Beakman's electro-shocking fright wig, the star, 44, was a performance artist whose work won NEA and Guggenheim grants.

His coif, his emotive eyebrows, and his torso-shaking chuckle were the subject of frequent parody when **Tom Snyder** hosted NBC's long-run post-Carson talk show, *Tomorrow*. Canceled in 1982 to make way for a comic named David Letterman, Snyder switched to radio. But at 58, the veteran returned to television in *The Late Late Show with Tom Snyder*, which fittingly followed Letterman on CBS's late-night schedule.

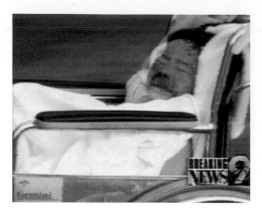

A day-care center lost 15 toddlers; 153 adults also died when the worst terrorist attack in modern U.S. history destroyed a high-rise federal office building in Oklahoma City. The act was perpetrated not by foreign radicals, but rather someone as homebrewed as the explosives he packed in a rented truck: 27-year-old ex-G.I. Timothy McVeigh.

So what if *Dances with Wolves* led some to refer to him as a Sioux named Boy; **Kevin Costner**'s 1990 epic won seven of the 11 Oscars for which it was nominated. In *500 Nations*, his first primetime project, the 40- year-old star (here with director **Jack Leustig**) served as host of a four-night, eight-hour documentary that examined the diverse cultures of the first Americans.

· · · · · · · · · · ·

FRAN DRESCHER

On starring in her own series, The Nanny:

"When I was a little girl growing up in Flushing, Queens, eight o'clock on CBS was my magic hour. No more homework, no more 'clean your room,' just one hour that dreams are made of. Thank you, CBS, for making this little girl's dreams come true. Oy, do I sound sentimental or what?"

Bill Clinton defeats Bob Dole to retain the presidency. Paris-bound TWA Flight 800 explodes in midair, probably from a spark in its fuel tank; 230 die. Theodore Kaczynski, 53, is arrested and charged with the Unabombings that, over 18 years, killed three and maimed 20. Prince Charles and Princess Diana of Great Britain are divorced.

Premiering series: *Cosby* (CBS); *Early Edition* (CBS); *Everybody Loves Raymond* (CBS); *King of the Hill* (FOX); *Nash Bridges* (CBS); *Promised Land* (CBS); *The Rosie O'Donnell Show* (SYND); *Spin City* (ABC); *3rd Rock from the Sun* (NBC).

Movies: *The English Patient* (Oscar); *Fargo*; *Independence Day*; *Jerry Maguire*; *Scream*; *Twister*; *Welcome to the Dollhouse*.

Songs: "Because You Loved Me" (Celine Dion); "Counting Blue Cars" (Dishwalla); "Tha Crossroads" (Bone Thugs-N-Harmony); "Killing Me Softly with His Song" (Fugees); "Macarena" (Los Del Rio); "1979" (Smashing Pumpkins).

Books: *Angela's Ashes* (Frank McCourt); *Primary Colors* (Anonymous, aka Joe Klein).

Died: comedian George Burns, 100; singer Ella Fitzgerald, 79; composer Jonathan (*Rent*) Larson, 35; actor Marcello Mastroianni, 72; actress Audrey Meadows, 69; actor Howard Rollins, 46; astronomer Carl Sagan, 62; rap's Tupac Shakur, 25.

Debuts: Element 112, still unnamed; olestra, a "fat-free" fat; Tickle Me Elmo doll.

Bill Cosby could easily banish his grumpiness from being pensioned off, as when pal **Doug E. Doug** won a chance at a half-court shot worth $1 million. The sitcom *Cosby*, which reunited the 59-year-old comedian with Phylicia Rashad, his leading lady of eight years, also costarred Madeline Kahn. In 1998 Cosby would add a second primetime show, an updated version of *Kids Say the Darndest Things*.

America was on heightened security alert in the days preceding the Summer Olympics in Atlanta. Thus when a Paris-bound 747 exploded in midair soon after leaving New York, suspicion fell on a terrorist's bomb or missile. Experts would conclude, though, that the 230 aboard TWA Flight 800 most likely died because a spark from a faulty wiring system ignited fuel-tank vapors.

The Millionaire's Marvin Miller used to arrive with a life-altering check. *Early Edition*'s **Kyle Chandler** (right center) arrived with something more precious than money: life-saving news gleaned from a copy of the next day's newspaper, which came only to his door. The hour-long series costarred Shanesia Davis and **Fisher Stevens** (far right).

His new climate dictated a new wardrobe—pea jackets instead of pastel T-shirts—and the nearest Bay was San Francisco, not Biscayne. Not to worry. **Don Johnson**, 46, returned to primetime seven years after *Miami Vice* to portray *Nash Bridges*, an SFPD detective who often buddied up on cases with **Cheech Marin**'s ex-cop.

291

The 38th running of the Daytona 500, the race that traditionally launches the NASCAR season, was captured by Dale Jarrett. To better track the stock cars through their 150 mph-plus laps, CBS Sports deployed FlyingCam, a miniature helicopter rigged with video.

Though married with three tots and gainfully employed as a sportswriter, **Ray Romano** still suffered separation anxieties—he was anxious to separate from meddlesome parents **Doris Roberts** and **Peter Boyle.** The sitcom *Everybody Loves Raymond* costarred Patricia Heaton and Brad Garrett.

In
Their
Own
Words

. . . .

BILL
COSBY

*Who joined CBS
and revitalized its
Monday night
comedy lineup:*

"I wish I could
have done more
for my network."

A fter 156 years, Britain returns control of Hong Kong to China. Teething pains: boxer Mike Tyson gnaws foe Evander Holyfield's ear; sportscaster Marv Albert bites a sex partner's back. U.S. cigarette makers offer to settle a legion of lawsuits for $370 billion.

Premiering series: *Ally McBeal* (FOX); *Brooklyn South* (CBS); *Buffy the Vampire Slayer* (WB); *George and Leo* (CBS); *The Gregory Hines Show* (CBS); *Just Shoot Me* (NBC); *Michael Hayes* (CBS); *Nothing Sacred* (ABC); *The Practice* (ABC); *Public Eye* (CBS); *Veronica's Closet* (NBC).

Movies: *Boogie Nights*; *Face/Off*; *The Full Monty*; *Good Will Hunting*; *L.A. Confidential*; *Men in Black*; *Titanic*.

Songs: "Bitch" (Meredith Brooks); "Blue" (LeAnn Rimes); "Candle in the Wind 1997" (Elton John); "MMMbop" (Hanson); "Shy" (Ani DiFranco); "Wannabe" (The Spice Girls); "Where Have All the Cowboys Gone" (Paula Cole).

Books: *Cold Mountain* (Charles Frazier); *The Perfect Storm* (Sebastian Junger); *Underworld* (Don DeLillo).

Died: singer John Denver, 53; Diana, Princess of Wales, 36; journalist Charles Kuralt, 62; actor Toshiro Mifune, 77; actor Robert Mitchum, 79; singer Laura Nyro, 49; comic Red Skelton, 84; humanitarian Mother Teresa, 87.

Debuts: mammal cloned from adult cell (Dolly the sheep); Tamagotchi virtual pet.

Judd Hirsch's arrival had an unsettling effect on **Bob Newhart**, here uncharacteristically grappling with **Jason Bateman**. In *George and Leo*, Newhart's fourth CBS sitcom, he played a bookseller who through son Bateman's marriage acquired not only a daughter-in-law but also her deadbeat dad, Hirsch.

At Augusta a year earlier, **Tiger Woods**'s game had suffered because he was also cramming for sophomore-year exams at Stanford University. Now a full-time pro, he donned his signature Sunday red to shoot a final-round 69 and finish 18 strokes under par, 12 better than his nearest competitor—both records. The Masters was one of four tournaments the 21-year-old Woods would win in his first full year on tour.

No wedding in history was more watched than hers. Sixteen momentous years later—after she had borne a future King of England, tamed her personal demons, shaken the House of Windsor by daring to divorce the Prince of Wales, and become a champion of unfashionable causes— no funeral in history was more watched than hers. Fatally injured in an automobile accident in Paris, **Princess Diana** was 36.

Danny Aiello wasn't exactly proposing a toast to good health when he clinked Chianti glasses in *Mario Puzo's The Last Don*. The actor, 64, played the head of an extended Family that included Joe Mantegna, Kirstie Alley, and Jason Gedrick; Daryl Hannah and Penelope Ann Miller became members by proxy. The six-hour miniseries left enough business unfinished to warrant a 1998 sequel, *The Last Don II*.

The newsmagazine show *Public Eye with Bryant Gumbel* marked the 49-year-old broadcaster's first primetime series. Although his journalistic beats had included presidential elections and the Olympics, **Gumbel**'s chief duty from 1982 until joining CBS was anchoring NBC's early-morning *Today* show. Among *Public Eye*'s correspondents: Bernie Goldberg, Peter Van Sant, and Rita Braver.

Arriving at a crime scene, **Michael DeLuise** (right) and **Titus Welliver** (left) initiated hot pursuit through the streets of *Brooklyn South*. The hour-long show followed their lives on duty and off, along with those of seven other young beat cops under the command of *Hill Street Blues* vet James B. Sikking.

In
Their
Own
Words

• • • • • • • • • •

ROMA
DOWNEY

and

DELLA
REESE

On two key reasons why viewers found Touched By An Angel *appealing:*

Downey: "Della is the universal mother. There is a genuine love between us."

Reese: "We have tried war. We have tried greed. We have tried technology. We have tried drugs. None of it works because none of it has a spiritual base."

Index to Photos

Author's Note

A book based on more than 385 evocative and culturally significant photographs from the past half-century is much easier to write than to research and assemble.

Without the unhesitating cooperation of the following individuals, this volume would have remained yet another neat idea whose time had not come.

Bruce Pomerantz, in spirit my coauthor, unearthed the oft-glorious images—some unseen for decades—by patiently combing through the CBS Photo Archive.

His formidable endeavor was made more bearable by the support and encouragement he received from Gail Plautz, John Filo, and Vika Zahn of CBS Photography; by the assistance of researchers Marion Bodine and Stefani Cunningham; and by the computer expertise of David Russell.

At CBS News Archives, Doug McKinney, Toni Gavin, and Hector Perez isolated video images of historic events that were then digitized by Joan Johnson and Ned Steinberg of CBS Operations & Engineering. The rights to the video images of athletic events were cleared by Deanna O'Toole of CBS Sports.

Gil Schwartz and Michael G. Silver of CBS Communications were instrumental in helping me decode the network's rich history and corporate culture, and also vetted my copy for accuracy. Even more than those vital contributions, I appreciate the complete editorial freedom they so generously granted me.

For conceiving this book and for bringing me onto it, I thank Judy Bass of CBS Enterprises/Business Affairs; Jeffrey Nemerovski (who in addition smoothed the inevitable moments of panic with great forbearance) and Ken Ross of CBS Consumer Products; and Quay Hays of General Publishing Group.

If these pages capture most of the key milestones of the network's 50 years of programming, it is due in large measure to the guidance furnished by Ray Faiola and John Behrens of CBS Audience Services; Margery Baker and Hal Lewis of CBS News Productions; Barbara Hunter-Welsh of CBS Daytime Programs; and Ray Harmon of CBS Sports. Valuable counsel was also rendered by Terry Botwick of CBS Entertainment and Kathy Broyles of CBS Television Network/Advertising & Promotion.

I could not have written so confidently without the research provided by Steve Reichl and by Laura Kapnick and Carole Parnes of CBS Reference Library.

Peter Hoffman of General Publishing Group orchestrated the complex transformation of images and text into a bound volume. Dana Granoski, with whom I worked in Santa Monica, executed the design with great sensitivity; Steve Baeck and Carolyn Wendt made sure I wrote what I meant; and Bill Castillo, Bill Neary, Dave Chadderdon, Russel Lockwood, and Tom Archibeque graciously sweated myriad production details.

Finally, to Sallie Gouverneur and Erika Bai Siebels, Norman Snyder, and especially Dick Stolley: many thanks.

Tony Chiu
April 1998